J500

A Young Scientist's Guide to defying DISASTERS

A Young Scientist's Guide to defying DISASTERS

GIBBS SMITH

with skill & daring

JAMES DOYLE

Illustrations by ANDREW BROZYNA

Manufactured in China in May 2012 by Toppan

First Edition
16 15 14 13 12   5 4 3 2

Published by
Gibbs Smith
P.O. Box 667
Layton, Utah 84041

1.800.835.4993 orders
www.gibbs-smith.com

Design and illustrations by Andrew J. Brozyna
Gibbs Smith books are printed on either recycled, 100% post-consumer waste,
FSC-certified papers or on paper produced from sustainable PEFC-certified
forest/controlled wood source. Learn more at www.pefc.org.

Library of Congress Cataloging-in-Publication Data

Dolye, James, 1972–
  A young scientist's guide to defying disasters with skill and daring / James
Doyle ; illustrations by Andrew Brozyna. — 1st ed.
    p. cm.
  ISBN 978-1-4236-2440-0
  1. Science—Juvenile literature. I. Title.
  Q163.D69 2012
  500—dc23
                    2011039879

For Oonágh, Conall, Erin and Cara
Thanks to Suzie Napayok for translations

Contents

Warning!

STOP! right where you are. You now only have a few seconds to make your decision. You must decide here and now which direction your life is going to take you from here on. If you are squeamish in any way or a complete scaredy pants, then it's best if you put this book right back where you found it and walk away while you still can. Your nerves will not be able to hold out to the heart-pounding exploits within this book. On the other hand, if you have a thirst for adventure and dodging danger, and you're not easily scared, then welcome. You are now "in." You are now part of a very elite and specialized group. A group of explorers who, by the end of this book, will have the skills and know-how to master even the most dangerous situations on Earth.

Want to know how to survive the ravaging winds of a hurricane? Or how to survive a super tsunami? Would you like to be able to dodge pyroclastic bombs? Or hitch a ride on a lahar? If the answer to these questions is yes, then you've come to the right place because in your hand is your guide to surviving anything, anywhere, at anytime. You will not only learn how to combat the highest mountains and the deepest oceans, you will explore the freezing poles and sweltering deserts, and everything else in between. What's more, this is not just a survival manual—it's an insider guide to the science and mechanics of planet Earth. This is your guide to surviving anything from the four corners of the Earth. This is your guide to surviving anything Earth can throw at you! So, kit up, engage your brain and prepare yourself for the ride of a lifetime.

Natural
Catastrophes

Milky Seas

Milky seas are not really life-threatening, but they are a really cool and very rare natural phenomena that any intrepid explorer would be bursting to experience. Milky seas have long been recorded and described in maritime or oceangoing folklore. In the 18th century, these weird phenomena were written about in the Jules Verne classic novel, *20,000 Leagues Under the Sea*, but until recently there was no real scientific proof to back up the crazy claims of seafarers.

Many sailors would describe what they were experiencing as though they were "sailing upon a field of snow" or "gliding over a giant sea of milk," all of which was experienced in absolute darkness with not so much as the light of the moon.

The glowing waters appear to extend right out to the horizon in all directions and can last from several hours to several days.

More recently, it has been possible to gather clearer scientific evidence about milky seas. On the night of January 25, 1995, a British merchant vessel, the S.S. *Lima*, was sailing through the northwestern Indian Ocean off the coast of the African nation of Somalia, when it sailed into a milky sea. The ship's captain wanted the event recorded and so contacted the Naval Research Laboratory (or NRL for short). It was able to track the milky sea from space using a special satellite that can detect extremely low levels of visible light.

The satellite detected images of an enormous area of glowing water spanning over 6,000 mi^2, or approximately 15,000 km^2 (that's the same surface area as the entire State of Connecticut in the United States). The glowing continued for three whole nights. The cause of these strange nighttime events is still being discussed, but scientists believe they are linked to strong bioluminescence (which is science-speak for natural biological light). The light is thought to be produced by huge colonies of bacteria in surface waters. In other words, this is the ocean's own version of billions upon billions of tiny fireflies grouping and glowing together. Those guys are a real bunch of bright sparks!

IF YOU ARE PLANNING AN EXPEDITION TO DISCOVER A MILKY SEA, YOU WILL NEED THE FOLLOWING:

1. A seaworthy oceangoing vessel, aka, a boat

2. A reliable and experienced crew (easily recruited with a palm of silver)

3. Sufficient food and fuel for a long expedition

4. An awful lot of luck! (Remember, these events are extremely rare and only the most daring and fortunate explorers have encountered them.)

YOUNG SCIENTIST ACTIVITY
How to Make Water Glow

This experiment will allow you to make glowing water.

EQUIPMENT NEEDED:

A bottle of tonic water

A fluorescent highlighter

A very dark room

An ultraviolet black light (which can be picked up cheaply at most stores)

INSTRUCTIONS:

1. Take a fluorescent highlighter pen. Be careful to break it open and remove the felt tip inside. Now soak the felt in a glass of water for several minutes.

2. Take the glass of water and UV black light into a very dark room.

3. Turn on the UV black light near your water and get ready, set, glow!

Science Factoid

The fluorescent highlighter and the tonic water both contain phosphors, which are special substances that give out light and have the ability to make ultraviolet light that is usually invisible to the human eye, visible. The UV black light and the phosphors combine to make the water glow. Tonic water also works because the UV light reacts with phosphors in a chemical within the tonic water called quinine.

Limnic Eruptions
(aka, exploding lakes)

Now don't get scared, limnic eruptions are very, very rare natural disasters and it is highly unlikely that you will ever encounter such an event, but it is best to be prepared.

These extraordinary occurrences happen when large amounts of carbon dioxide (CO_2) and other gases suddenly erupt from deep lakes and can result in the suffocation of wildlife, livestock, and even humans. Lakes in which such activity occurs may be known as limnically active lakes or "exploding" lakes—BOOM!!!

WHAT YOU SHOULD KNOW:

1. For a lake to explode it must be almost completely saturated with a gas. In the two recorded cases that have been observed, the major component was carbon dioxide. The CO_2 may come from volcanic gases emitted under the lake or from decomposition of organic material.

2. Before a lake is saturated, it behaves just like a fizzy drink: the CO_2 is dissolved in the water. In both the lake and the soft drink, CO_2 dissolves much more easily when it is at a higher pressure. This is why bubbles in a can of soda only form after the drink is opened; the pressure is released and the gas comes out of the drink.

3. Meanwhile, back at the lake, once saturated all you need is a trigger for all this pressurized gas to be released. Scientists say any natural event will do the trick, such as a volcanic eruption or landslide; however, something as minor as wind or rain can trigger it.

4. Once an eruption occurs, a large CO_2 cloud forms above the lake and begins to expand into the surrounding region. As CO_2 is denser or "heavier" than air, it has a tendency to sink to the ground while pushing up any breathable air. As a result, any life forms that need to breathe oxygen suffocate once the CO_2 cloud reaches them, as there is no breathable air (this is not good news if you are present at an eruption!). Furthermore, the CO_2 can make human bodily fluids very acidic, potentially causing CO_2 poisoning. As victims gasp for air, they actually hurt themselves more by sucking in even more CO_2.

SURVIVAL TIPS

Fortunately, these events are exceedingly rare and have only been knowingly observed twice. So, you are fairly safe, but just in case—you should do the following:

1. When visiting an area that has a limnically active lake, you should check if there is a de-gassing procedure in place. Some, but not all, explosive lakes actually have the CO_2 removed. This is carried out using a very simple siphoning technique: A pipe is positioned vertically in the lake with its upper end above the water's surface. Water saturated with CO_2 enters the bottom of the pipe and rises to the top. The lower pressure at the surface allows the gas to come out of the solution. (It's a bit like putting a giant straw at the bottom of the lake and sucking out the gas.) This technique will keep the CO_2 at safe levels.

2. If you are unfortunate enough to be close to an exploding lake at the time of an eruption, you should make your way to higher ground as soon as possible. The CO_2 released is heavier than the surrounding oxygen and therefore "hugs" the ground and forces the oxygen above it. Find the nearest hill or tree and climb—you should be safe at any height above 10 ft./3 m.

3. Get an early warning system! CO_2 detection equipment can be expensive. A more cost-effective and fun technique is to invest in a pet mouse. Mice have the ability to detect CO_2 and it makes them crazy! Excess CO_2 in the air signals danger for mice, whether it's because too many animals are breathing in too cramped a space or a hungry predator is about to exhale down its furry neck. Either way, your little furry friend could save your skin.

YOUNG SCIENTIST ACTIVITY
Raisin' Raisins

In this activity, you're not actually growing raisins from scratch but you are "raising" the raisins up using some very clever science.

EQUIPMENT NEEDED:

A can of clear soda such as Sprite or 7up

A box of raisins

A large glass

INSTRUCTIONS:

1. Pour the can of soda into the glass until it's almost full.

2. Take a handful of raisins and drop them into the glass.

3. They should immediately sink, but wait a few seconds and see what happens.

Science Factoid

The fizz you see in a soda is a gas called CO_2. It's jam-packed with so much CO_2 that it does not take much to cause it to come back out again. The surface of the raisins traps tiny bubbles of air when they are dropped into the glass. These tiny bubbles collect CO_2 from the soda and begin to grow. When the bubbles grow large enough, they begin to lift the raisins to the top of the glass. This is similar to the gaseous release that happens in the lake.

Tsunamis

You pronounce tsunami, "soo-nahm-ee." It is a Japanese word that means "harbor wave."

A tsunami is a series of huge waves that are caused by movements under the sea, such as an earthquake or an underwater volcano eruption. The waves travel like ripples on a pond in exactly the same way they would if you had just thrown a rock into it, and they can travel at great speeds to hit the shore. Anyone who is in the path of a tsunami is in great danger. Here's how to recognize the signs of a tsunami and how to protect yourself.

THINGS NOT TO DO

Don't try to outrun the waves. They travel very much faster than you and much faster than your car can! They can travel at speeds of up to 450 mi./800 km an hour. (That's pretty fast!)

Don't be fooled that the waves in a tsunami are not that big. Waves from a tsunami can be as high as 80 ft./25 m. They only grow bigger as they get to the shore. This means that they can start off as just a ripple of water in the middle of the ocean and become bigger and bigger until they become a gigantic wave when they hit the shore.

Whatever you do, don't climb a tree unless you have absolutely no other choice. Trees often snap under the pressure of the water and a tsunami can generate a huge volume of water. If you have to climb a tree, find a very strong and tall one and climb as high as you can.

Don't get confused—often in movies, tsunamis are commonly mixed-up with tidal waves. Tsunamis are caused by eruptions or earthquakes and have nothing to do with tides.

THINGS TO DO

Keep away from the beach! Do not go anywhere near the beach or into buildings near the beach. Even if you see just a small tsunami, leave immediately. Tsunami waves grow bigger and continue to hit, so the next giant wave may be on the way. The series of waves are also called "the wave train."

Find higher ground. Go up a hill or to a higher area of the town or city. If you are trapped, find a tall, strong building and climb to the top of it, maybe even sit on its roof.

Leave your possessions. Your survival is more important than toys, books and other things. Leave them behind and get to safety.

Stay away for several hours. A tsunami can continue to hit the shore for many hours, so the danger may not be over for a while. Do not return to the area until you get an "all-clear" message from emergency services. If you do not get this message, wait patiently.

Find a radio and keep tuned in for updates.

If you get caught in the water, the most important thing is to keep afloat. Grab onto anything that floats, such as a tree trunk, a piece of a building that is floating, etc. Use the floating object to get you near something you can climb up onto and get out of the water if possible.

NATURE'S EARLY WARNING SYSTEM

If you live near the sea or are on holiday there, nature will give you some very clear warning signs:

- There may be an earthquake or the ground rumbles.

- The sea itself suddenly pulls back and leaves bare sand, making the beach seem like it has grown a lot larger.

- Local animals begin to behave in a strange manner. They suddenly leave, gather in large groups, or try to get to higher ground. (Follow that elephant!)

Maelstroms

This is a tough one, and unless you are fully equipped, it is going to be extremely difficult to defy one of these. Even when fully prepared, the odds are against you. However, preparation is key and if you do run into one of these babies, you want to give yourself the best possible chance of survival.

WHAT ARE MAELSTROMS?

The word "maelstrom" is a Scandinavian word meaning "grinding current." Maelstroms are very powerful whirlpools or swirling bodies of water with incredibly powerful downdrafts. Imagine a stormy, raging sea and add in the twisting vortex of a tornado. Only then can you begin to understand why sailors of old feared them so much and why their reputation grew to mythical status. The fear of getting trapped in a maelstrom before being sucked down to impending doom is still strong today.

Cynics argue that stories of sailors losing their lives and boats being destroyed are greatly exaggerated and even completely fictional; however, more recent scientific and documentary research seems to support the fearsome reputation of the mighty maelstrom.

MIGHTY MAELSTROMS

Here are just a few of Earth's meanest maelstroms:

The Saltstraumen maelstrom is found about 48 mi./30 km off the coast of Norway. Near the Arctic Circle, it is the mightiest maelstrom on the planet and creates the strongest tidal currents on the globe. The turbulent waters can reach speeds of 25 mi./40 km per hour as hundreds of thousands of gallons of seawater are "funneled" through a very narrow strait. So dangerous is this area of water that there is only a small window of time each day when larger ships can sail through.

Although, Saltstraumen is the world's strongest maelstrom, the Moskstraumen is the most famous one, mentioned in many books and movies. Located off the Lofoten Islands, in Norway, Moskstraumen is the second-strongest whirlpool in the world with powerful currents that reach speeds of nearly 20 mi./32 km per hour.

NOISY NATURE

Some maelstroms not only create some of the most dangerous waters on Earth but also some of the loudest. The third-largest maelstrom in the world is located in the relatively narrow strait of Corryvreckan on the western coast of Scotland. It can generate wave swells of up to 30 ft./9 m, but, more interestingly, the noise generated by these waters is so loud it can be heard up to 10 mi./16 km away. At one time, the

British navy classed the waters as "unsailable" before downgrading them to "extremely dangerous."

Similarly, the Old Sow maelstrom situated between New Brunswick and Maine earned its name from the "pig-like" screeching sounds that occur when the full fury of this vortex is heard. Smaller whirlpools on all sides of Old Sow are nicknamed "the piglets." OINK! OINK!

TRIVIA Researchers in Scotland once tossed a mannequin equipped with a life jacket into the Corryvreckan maelstrom. They wanted to test the tall tales of seafarers that maelstroms would suck humans down into the sea's depths to their eventual doom. The mannequin entered the vortex and disappeared. When it was later recovered, the dive meter showed that it had been sucked down to more than 600 ft./183 m deep and the life jacket was full of gravel. This was clear evidence that the dummy had been scraped along the sea floor.

SURVIVAL TIPS

I think it's very apparent that maelstroms shouldn't be messed with. They are extremely powerful, noisy and very unpredictable. If you are unlucky enough to encounter one, here are a few survival tips:

1. Only travel out to a maelstrom with experienced local sailors and divers. They will know the waters better than anyone else and will be your best chance of getting through one.

2. If you are sailing through a maelstrom, it is best to do it when the waters are calmest. Most have what experts call a "time window" when it's safest to do so.

3. If you are going to dive near a maelstrom (which is not a very wise idea), you need to be fully equipped with a proper diving suit and a sufficient supply of air in case you run into difficulties. You will most likely need a gas mixture instead of traditional compressed air. This will allow you to swim deeper for longer.

Beware, though, the normal limit of recreational diving is around 150–160 ft./46–49 m. If you get caught up in the depths of a maelstrom's vortex, you could be swept down to much greater depths. Here, increased nitrogen levels will knock you unconscious, and the oxygen you are breathing will become toxic and the air you breathe will kill you.

YOUNG SCIENTIST ACTIVITY
Make Your Own Maelstrom

With just a few items, it is fairly straightforward to make a manageable maelstrom that works on pretty much the same principle as the real thing.

EQUIPMENT NEEDED:

A see-through plastic bottle

A tube of glitter

Dishwashing soap

INSTRUCTIONS:

1. Add water to your see-through bottle until it's about three-quarters full.

2. Drop in one or two squirts of dish soap.

3. Drop in some glitter.

4. Screw a cap onto your bottle.

5. Hold your bottle upside down and shake it round and round in a circular movement. What do you see?

Science Factoid

The circular motion of you shaking the bottle sets up a spinning force or vortex. It is these types of forces that create the real-life maelstroms. The glitter you added simply makes it easier to see the motion of the water.

Tidal Bores

Despite the name, tidal bores are anything but boring. They can be very dangerous and also very confusing, so the untrained explorer can be forgiven for being disorientated by one of nature's clever tricks. Remain focused as you prepare yourself for another of Earth's surprises.

WHAT IS A TIDAL BORE AND WHAT CAUSES IT?

Tidal bores are very large waves that can surge up a river from the sea. Crazy as it sounds, these beauties appear to work against gravity and basically reverse the natural flow of the river.

There are roughly sixty rivers across the planet that experience fairly regular tidal bores. They only occur at certain times of the year and are linked to flood tides, which are the highest tides caused when the sun and moon are aligned, creating a huge gravitational pull. This "pull" literally throws water inland and forces large waves of water from the sea up through the river channel.

SURVIVAL TIPS

1. Get a good spot—not only can bores be dangerous, they are also hugely popular to view. When a tidal bore is due, it is best to get a safe vantage point that is close enough to give you a good view but not close enough that you get swept up in the wave.

2. Listen up! The very nature of a tidal bore means they have their own "roar." Some can be heard from miles away. As the wave moves upstream and gets "funneled" inland, the water gets churned up violently, creating a lot of noise and acting as an early warning system.

3. Surf's up! Some tidal bores are smoother and less violent than others. These often attract "bore surfers" who arrive with kayaks, surfboards or boogie boards to ride the bore inland. So, if you want to surf a bore, it's time to kit up!

TRIVIA   For more than 2,000 years, people have gathered at rivers with tidal bores to "bore watch." Be careful though! Many people have died from drowning while watching bores.

WORLD'S LARGEST BORE

The Qiantang River in China has the world's largest tidal bore. It can generate a wave that's 30 ft./9 m high.

SOME REALLY BORE-ING NAMES (NOT)

Tidal bores are such spectacular events that some have generated their own legendary nicknames. These include "The Seven Ghosts" in Indonesia, "The Great Roar" in South America and "The Black Dragon" in China.

YOUNG SCIENTIST ACTIVITY
Magic Finger Experiment

This clever but simple experiment is very easy to follow and a cool way to play with science.

EQUIPMENT NEEDED:

A bowl

Some Water

Dish detergent

Black pepper

INSTRUCTIONS:

1. Fill the bowl with water.

2. Shake the black pepper across the top of the water.

3. Place your finger in the water. What happens? (Nothing much, eh?)

4. Now, put a little detergent on your finger and dip it into the pepper and water. Notice how the pepper moves away from you and toward the edges of the bowl.

Science Factoid

Water has a surface tension that makes it rise up and bulge at the top. When the detergent comes in contact with the water, it lowers the surface tension a little and the water begins to spread out. As the water "flattens," it carries the pepper with it toward the outer edges of the bowl. Tidal bores are caused by a similar phenomena—high spring tides and gravity create a bulge in the ocean, which "flattens" when it enters a river, carrying a wave with it.

Violent Volcanoes

The word "volcano" is taken from the name of Vulcan, the god of fire in Roman mythology. The Romans and many other civilizations witnessed the deadly power of volcanoes. They also discovered that volcanoes could destroy, burn and submerge both people and places in a much greater variety of ways than other natural hazards, and even today we are still drawn to live in these danger zones. First we need to look at how and where they form.

HOW A VOLCANO IS MADE

Most volcanoes are found along tectonic plate margins, which are long lines that divide the Earth's surface, which is a little bit like the outside of a hardboiled egg after it has been cracked with a spoon. A volcano is formed when liquid rock or magma shoots out or erupts through the ground. Once above the ground, the liquid is then called lava, but the type of lava erupted varies greatly and can have very different effects. The viscosity of the lava (scientist-speak for how thick or runny it is) depends on the type of rock that is melted and the pressure within the volcano. Some lava is thick like jam while others are runny like thin, watery custard. As the lava cools, it hardens, forming new rock and eventually a whole mountain or volcano.

There are two main groups of eruptions. First are those that are dominated by lava and tend to be found at "constructive" plates, which allow basalt to rise freely to the surface. The second group are those dominated by ash and smoke, which is normally found at what experts call "destructive" plate margins where the material erupted is typically pyroclastic (I will brief you on this later). These differing eruptions, and other factors, result in very different-shaped volcanoes.

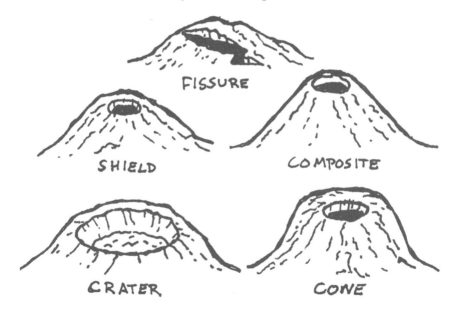

FISSURE

SHIELD

COMPOSITE

CRATER

CONE

WHICH TYPE OF CONE WOULD YOU LIKE?

Many volcano varieties exist and can be grouped by cone shape. The table below shows the main types:

CONE SHAPE	FEATURES
Fissure volcano	Gentle slopes; they are found at constructive ocean plates. The lava is runny and can flow over large distances.
Shield volcano	Gentle slopes but steeper than fissure because of repeated explosions and the continuous build up of lava layers.
Composite volcano	These are large and old volcanoes made up of both ash and lava.
Crater, aka Caldera, volcano	These are formed during very violent eruptions normally after there has been a large buildup of gas beneath the volcano. Often these volcanoes have large, blown-out craters caused by explosive eruptions.
Cone volcano	These volcanoes have symmetrical sides but the types vary depending on whether ash was erupted or viscous lava.

VERY VIOLENT VOLCANOES

Between the 10th and 12th of April 1815, the Tambora volcano in Indonesia erupted, killing around 92,000 people. This is believed to be the most deadly eruption in history and produced ash fall, a tsunami and, later, widespread disease and starvation.

Between the 26th and 28th of August 1883, the Krakatoa volcano in Indonesia erupted. This was the second most deadly volcano ever recorded, and it killed an estimated 36,000 people. This eruption also generated a huge tsunami and the ash cloud blanked out the sun.

Mauna Loa in Hawaii is the largest live volcano on Earth. One of its eruptions lasted one and a half years, and it is actually the tallest mountain on Earth but is not classed as such because most of it is underwater.

TRIVIA   HOTTER! COLDER! HOTTER AGAIN! In Pucón, Chile, crazy bungee jumpers will launch themselves from a helicopter down into the crater of an active volcano. They are flown directly overhead before diving some 460 ft./ 140 m toward the volcano's molten lava.

HOTSPOTS

Some volcanoes form well away from plate margins, which confused "volcanologists" (the scientific word for people who study volcanoes) for a very long time.

These volcanoes, mostly in the chain of the Hawaiian Islands, were nowhere near the places where volcanoes usually form. Later scientists discovered hotspots beneath the Earth's crust that are superheated and cause magma to melt through the crust and gradually start building a volcano.

THE WAYS IN WHICH A VOLCANO CAN GET YOU!

Volcanic events can produce many different effects, so much so that they are grouped into primary and secondary.

Primary Effects

Tephra (pronounced "Tef-Raa")—This is volcanic ash that is bigger than 2 mm in size. Anything smaller is classed as ash. It is normally erupted when magma breaks up due to explosions. It causes breathing difficulties and even suffocation, and can ground airplanes when their engines clog up with the ash.

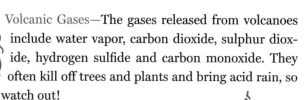

Volcanic Gases—The gases released from volcanoes include water vapor, carbon dioxide, sulphur dioxide, hydrogen sulfide and carbon monoxide. They often kill off trees and plants and bring acid rain, so watch out!

Lava Flows—These destroy pretty much everything in their path. Fortunately, you can walk or drive away from them. These are actually the least life threatening.

Secondary Effects

If you think that having defied the above you will be okay, you must think again—these are only the beginning. You've also got lahars, volcanic landslides, tsunamis (page 11) and jökulhlaups.

"Jökulhlaup" (pronounced "yoke-uhl-howp") is the Icelandic word for dangerous floods. "Jökul" is the Icelandic word for glacier and the "hlaup" part means a flood. In other words, this is a really dangerous flood that happens when volcanoes erupt beneath glaciers. The sudden release of heat quickly melts the glacier and releases huge amounts of fast-flowing water.

Almost 60 percent of volcanic eruptions in Iceland occur beneath glacial ice. When they do, magma as hot as 2,192° F/1,200° C meets ice and boiling water. This creates an initial explosion of ice and fragmented rocks and then creates a sky full of electricity, toxic chemicals and ash! On the ground, the flowing river of water and debris can wipe out towns, bridges and power lines. In 1996, an eruption of the Grímsvötn volcano in Iceland caused a piece of glacier 4 mi. long, 328 ft. deep/6 km long, 100 m deep to melt. (That's a lot of melting ice cubes!)

Back in 1918, an eruption at the Katla volcano caused steam to combine with tiny particles that poured out of the eruption, creating high static charges. This in turn caused lightning strikes several times a second. This phenomenon is reported to have caused the electrocution and death of hundreds of livestock grazing nearby.

A similar event to a jökulhlaups is a lahar. These are volcanic mudflows of ash and debris that have mixed with water. Basically, they are giant volcanic mudflows and occur when a volcanic eruption coincides with heavy rain or mixes with river water. This hot mixture can travel at great speeds. On steep slopes, speeds can reach up to 63 mi./101 km per hour! I know . . . this is not good! The truth is, you most likely won't be able to outrun one of these. Lahars actually grow as they flow by picking up more rocks, vegetation and debris as they move. If a lahar gets you, it will sweep you away, suffocate you and then entomb you as the mud starts to solidify.

In 1985, the eruption of the Nevado del Ruiz volcano in Colombia caused a lahar that ripped through the town of Armero, killing more than 23,000 people in one night.

SURVIVAL TIPS

In truth, these are very fast moving and often provide little warning but here are some steps to take for survival:

1. Listen for local reports of imminent volcanic eruptions. Volcanoes are one of the hazards that give out a number of warning signs, including releasing gas and making local water more acidic. They also begin to release smoke and ash, the temperatures rise near the volcano, and scientists can even monitor the swelling or "bulging" in a volcano when it is due to erupt.

2. In the case of a lahar, one ingredient in the mix is heavy rain. Check local forecasts to ensure your expedition doesn't coincide with a report for rain.

3. If you can plan your base while exploring a jökulhlaup or lahar-prone region, set up camp high on valley sides or away from the natural flow of water. This will ensure that the water and mud are diverted away from you.

4. If all else fails and you only have a short time to escape, don't try to outrun it because you won't be able to. Jump in any kind of vehicle and drive.

YOUNG SCIENTIST ACTIVITY
Build a Lava Lamp

Many people wonder how the blobs and shapes in a lava lamp work. The answer is due to very basic scientific principles. This activity will show you how to make your very own lava lamp.

EQUIPMENT NEEDED:

One bottle of vegetable oil • One large clear soda bottle

Alka-Seltzer tablets • One cup of water

Food coloring • One funnel

INSTRUCTIONS:

1. Pour the cup of water into the bottle.

2. Now pour the bottle of vegetable oil into the bottle until it's almost full.

3. Drop in a lot of drops of food coloring.

4. Take half an Alka-Seltzer and drop it into the bottle and watch things start to move!

Science Factoid

The oil and colored water do not mix, and this keeps the blobs of color and oil separated. The Alka-Seltzer tablet falls to the bottom of the bottle and begins fizzing. This breathes life into your bottle by creating air bubbles that rise to the top of the bottle, taking colored water with them. At the top of the bottle, the gas escapes and the water falls back to the bottom. You can keep the movement going by adding new tablets to your bottle.

Quicksand

Any explorer worth his or her salt needs to be equipped to deal with unforeseen circumstances, and quicksand is a classic example of the hidden hazards adventurers have had to contend with since the times of cavemen. Moviemakers have long made us believe that quicksand is an undefeatable force of nature, while others have made out that it's a living organism in itself. Neither of these myths is true, but you do need to know more about this strange substance and how it acts to defy it.

WHAT IS QUICKSAND?

Quicksand can be found pretty much anywhere on the planet where the right conditions exist. You obviously need sand, but also a sufficient water supply to make the sand "super-saturated." This normally happens where sand is held in a "pocket" made out of clay or any other material that does not allow water to drain away easily. This pocket of sand and water will appear like a solid material at first glance, but will act like a liquid when stepped on, and that's one of its key dangers. If you do find yourself sinking into your worst nightmare, here are a few survival tips to help you out.

SURVIVAL TIPS

1. Pressure is critical to surviving quicksand. Light pressure allows the quicksand to move like a liquid, whereas, heavy pressure causes the sand-water mixture to act as a solid. When an explorer steps on it lightly, the quicksand liquefies and the feet of the explorer begin to sink into it.

2. Don't worry about getting sucked down into quicksand. Although you will sink when you first enter it, you will not sink over your head. At worst, you will end up chest deep. This is because humans are less dense than quicksand.

3. Don't panic! An untrained explorer will begin to thrash around quickly, hoping to break free, only to find that now the quicksand is acting like a solid, encasing him or her even more firmly in the unpredictable substance. The more you struggle in it, the faster you will sink. If you just relax, your body will float.

4. Remove your backpack. Try to remove your backpack as soon as you enter the quicksand. This can add to your total weight and pull you farther down.

5. Just add water. Keep a container of water with you. Adding water around your waist or a trapped limb helps the quicksand to act more like water and will speed your release.

YOUNG SCIENTIST ACTIVITY
Make Your Own Quicksand

EQUIPMENT NEEDED:

A large mixing bowl

One packet of cornstarch

A large spoon or wooden spoon

Some water

Two cups (equal sized)

INSTRUCTIONS:

1. The key to making the perfect quicksand is getting the thickness or consistency just right. First, take your large mixing bowl and pour in small amounts of water and cornstarch to form a mixture. You will use roughly ¼ more cornstarch than water. For every cup of water you mix in, add 1¼ cups of cornstarch.

2. Now use your spoon to stir the mixture, starting slowly and then faster.

3. Stirring the mixture quickly will make it hard and allow you to punch or poke it quickly. This makes it act like a solid material. Stirring slowly will make your mixture more like a liquid. Presto! You've made your very own quicksand.

Science Factoid

Speed of movement is crucial in this experiment—if you move your hand slowly through your mixture, it will behave like a liquid. But if you try to move your hand through it quickly, it acts like a solid substance, which is just how real quicksand acts. This happens because the cornstarch grains are mixed up and can't slide over each other due to the lack of water between them. Stirring slowly allows more water to get in between the cornstarch grains, letting them slide over each other much more easily and behave just like real quicksand.

Massive Mountains

If freezing temperatures, complete isolation from everyone and the very strong possibility of your fingers and toes falling off sounds like fun, then mountains are the place for you! Earth's mountain ranges are jagged towers of rock that can stretch into the skies for miles. For centuries, man has tried to scale these hostile giants—some have succeeded but many have failed.

THE WORLD'S HIGHEST MOUNTAIN PEAKS

Check out how big our biggest mountains really are and where you'll find them, if you think you're tough enough!

MOUNTAIN	CONTINENT	HEIGHT
Everest	Asia	29,015 ft. (8,840 m)
Aconcagua	South America	22,841 ft. (6,962 m)
McKinley	North America	20,310 ft. (6,190 m)
Kilimanjaro	Africa	19,341 ft. (5,895 m)
Elbrus	Europe	18,510 ft. (5,642 m)
Vinson Massif	Antarctica	16,470 ft. (4,890 m)
Puncak Jaya	Australasia	16,024 ft. (4,884 m)

WHAT ARE MOUNTAINS MADE OF?

Mountains are created by the following:

Eruptions—At plate margins, repeated volcanic eruptions can create and build new mountains.

Folds—This is the most common type of "mountain-building" process and occurs when two continental plates crash into one another and cause the Earth's crust to buckle and fold upward.

Domes—These are rounded or dome-shaped mountains that have been forced up by large amounts of magma coming from the Earth's mantle.

Faults—Occurs where cracks or "faults" in the Earth's crust exist. The land near a fault will either rise or fall. If it rises, it creates what geographers call a "block mountain."

DO MOUNTAINS STILL GROW?

Yes! Some of the mountains on Earth are still growing and evidence has been found to show that they actually started out life at or below sea level. The Himalayas, the Alps and the Andes ranges have all been found to contain seashells dating back more than 18,000 years. The world's highest mountain, Everest, is believed to be growing at a rate of .5 cm a year (the length of your baby fingernail). Currently measured at 29,035 ft./8,848 m, it is quite possible that future conquerors of Everest will have to climb slightly farther than those who reached its peak in the past.

EROSION—THE TOOL THAT SHAPES, SCRAPES AND SMOOTHS A MOUNTAIN

Once uplift, or growth, of a mountain ends, the erosive power of wind, water and ice set to work to create the wide variety of shapes we see in the mountains around the world. Mountain experts can tell the difference between a cirque, an arête and a pyramidal peak but can you? Here's a quick guide:

Cirque—Meaning "circus" in French, is a hollow in the side of a mountain caused by a glacier tearing into it. It is said to be like a huge arena or a giant's armchair, which explains the circus link.

Arête—Meaning "fishbone" in French, is a thin, knife-like ridge of rock that can form when two glaciers erode side by side. The arête is a thin ridge of rock that is left separating the two valleys. Arêtes can also form when two glacial cirques erode toward one another.

Pyramidal peaks—Also known as "glacial horns," these are the jagged peaks and are formed when three or more cirques form on the sides of mountains. This makes them very steep and very dangerous.

CLIMBERS BEWARE!

If what you've heard so far hasn't put you off mountain climbing, then there's always altitude sickness, snow blindness, oh, and the one we mentioned earlier, frostbite!

Altitude Sickness

The percentage of oxygen in the atmosphere at sea level is about 21 percent, and, as the altitude increases, the percentage remains the same but the number of oxygen molecules per breath is greatly reduced. At 12,000 ft./3,600 m there are roughly 40 percent fewer oxygen molecules per breath so the body must adjust to having less oxygen available.

The most common cause of altitude sickness is going too high too fast. If you take your time, your body will adapt to the decrease in oxygen. This is called "acclimatizing" and roughly takes one to three days at specific altitudes. For example, if you climb to 12,000 ft./3,600 m and spend several days at that altitude, your body will acclimatize to that elevation. If you then climb to 13,000 ft./3,962 m, you must acclimatize again, and so on. If you don't take your time, then you've got trouble. Worst-case scenario, you're looking at SAMS or HAPE. (These might sound like the names given to lovable clowns, but they can be fatal!)

SAMS (Severe Acute Mountain Sickness) and HAPE (High Altitude Pulmonary Edema) both can cause tiredness and confusion but the latter can result in death.

Snow Blindness

This can be a nasty one! It is caused by UV (ultraviolet) radiation exposure, which is high in mountainous areas. The UV rays are reflected off sheets of snow or ice, but the higher you climb on a mountain the bigger your risk. Specialists say that at every thousand feet above sea level, the intensity of UV rays increases by 4 percent. This is because there is less atmospheric filtering at high altitudes.

You may not experience the symptoms right away. Your eyes may appear bloodshot and there may be a gradual increase in tears. Pain will gradually worsen and it may feel like there is grit in your eyes. Eyes may swell to such an extent that they shut, but eventually you will be able to see again as the symptoms subside—just be sure not to touch or rub your eyes!

Frostbite

Frostbite is the freezing of skin and other tissues. It can happen if you are exposed to temperatures below freezing without proper protection. Prevention of frostbite is straightforward by the use of appropriate clothing, keeping the extremities warm and dry, and by eating high-energy foods and warm drinks—good luck, explorer!

THE PRESIDENTS' ROCK

Mount Rushmore in South Dakota in the United States is a safer type of mountain in many ways, but it is truly unique because the huge rock face has the heads of four past presidents carved into it. Each of the massive monuments measures over 60 ft./18 m in height. That's just like having your photograph blown up and plastered onto an image as tall as four London double-decker buses stacked on top of one another!

A nice and easy way to remember the place and names of the presidents is with a clever mnemonic—a mnemonic (pronounced "new-mon-ic") is a cunning trick used by English teachers to help people remember lists or things. It works when you create a sentence using the same letters in the same order of the things you need to remember.

For example: My Really Heavy Wellies Just Love Rain, which stands for: Mount Rushmore Houses Washington Jefferson Lincoln Roosevelt.

BASIC KIT YOU'LL NEED IN THE MOUNTAINS

1. Never leave planning and packing to the last minute; pack a few days before your expedition. This will give you time to check for everything.

2. Dryness is critical. Pack your emergency survival gear into a separate, waterproof bag to ensure everything is together and not exposed to the elements. This is particularly important when packing the essentials for fire such as matches and straw.

3. Have the basics. All good explorers should carry a map of the area they are visiting and a compass (most cell phones now have one as standard).

4. Prioritize. The simplest way to remember all the things you need is to prioritize from the most essential items and work down. Food, fluids, warm clothing, hiking boots, etc., should be first on your agenda, and also include a first-aid kit.

5. Prepare for sun hazard. As mentioned earlier, snow blindness is common on mountaintops, but aside from sunglasses, you'll also need sunblock and lip balm.

6. Remember tools and emergency items. A Swiss Army Knife contains many items including a corkscrew and bottle opener. Pack other items as necessary such as ropes, harnesses and zip lines. Remember to pack mirrors and whistles in case you need to signal for help.

See you at the top!

Iceberg Assaults

S ome people don't really understand just how dangerous icebergs can be and many ignore them as uninteresting chunks of floating ice—giant ice cubes basically. But there is so much to learn about icebergs, and they can be deceptively dangerous.

Science Factoid

Did you know that icebergs can quite literally explode and shatter? In doing so, they fire extremely sharp shards of ice into the air around them in what can be huge natural explosions.

ICEBERGS FOR BEGINNERS

Here a few facts about icebergs:

- Icebergs start out life as part of a glacier. Glaciers are enormous bodies of ice and snow. They can be hundreds of miles long and thousands of feet deep.

- An iceberg occurs when an individual piece of ice separates from the glacier. This is what scientists call "calving"—a process that can also be dangerous to those nearby, since huge ice blocks crash into the ocean and generate enormous waves.

- Icebergs can float because they are less dense than water.

- Icebergs are classified into six different categories, with "growlers" being the smallest; then "bergy bits," which are about the size of an average house; and then the remaining four groups, which are simply small, medium, large and very large.

- The largest iceberg recorded in recent years broke off the Antarctica ice shelf in March 2000. Named by scientist as B-15, it was approximately 4,500 mi^2/11,655 km^2, which is almost the size of Connecticut.

IS YOUR ICEBERG ALL WHITE?

Believe it or not, icebergs come in different colors. Yes, this is not a joke! Although the majority of icebergs on the planet end up being white, they also come in blue and green.

Almost all icebergs on the planet start out blue, which is the color of glacial ice that has been greatly compressed. They begin to turn white after going through a couple of periods of repeated freezing and thawing.

A rarer sight are green bergs, which originate from Antarctica and get their strange color from coming into contact with dissolved minerals over hundreds of years.

SURVIVAL TIPS

Most of us know the story of the *Titanic,* which was described as being "unsinkable" when first built in Belfast, Ireland, only to be struck down by an iceberg on its first voyage in 1912. The ship brushed the side of an iceberg, ripping it open, sinking the ship and killing 1,500 people. Since then, huge strides have been made to ensure human survival against iceberg events:

1. The International Ice Patrol is a force that monitors waters deemed to be at threat from icebergs. It provides information and warning to vessels sailing in dangerous regions to ensure survival.

2. "Iceberg alley" off the coast of Newfoundland, Canada, is now identified as an area of major iceberg activity.

3. New technologies have reduced iceberg casualties in recent years. Ships now have radar systems that can detect icebergs even in thick fog.

4. Tracking and destroying—The U.S. Coast Guard has even put sensors on icebergs or spray painted them in order to track their movements. If an iceberg is thought to be too big or problematic, fighter planes can be deployed to drop bombs on them and blow them up.

5. The main dangers with icebergs are their odd shapes and the fact that most of their mass is below the water line, unseen to intrepid explorers and sailors. You may have heard the old saying: "It's just the tip of the iceberg." This refers to the fact that the tip you can see is actually only a small piece of the total berg. Most icebergs vary between this simple math equation: $\frac{1}{6}$ and $\frac{1}{9}$. In other words, the actual total size of

an iceberg can be estimated from the visible piece above the water mark and then multiplying this by 6 or 9 times. This will give you a good gauge of what you are dealing with.

6. Exploding icebergs—even without the use of bombs, icebergs can explode naturally. As they continue to melt, the internal structure can become too weak to support its own weight. This can result in very dramatic explosions of ice shards in all directions, so watch out!

7. If you do manage to overcome the dangers posed by icebergs and happen to secure one for yourself, don't count on hanging onto it for too long. Most icebergs will melt completely within three to six years.

Dastardly Deserts

Most people are downright daft about deserts. If you are one of these people, it's probably not your fault. Most likely it's due to a combination of terrible teachers, aimless authors and misguided moviemakers. You see, when someone says "desert," most of us automatically think of heat, sand, camels and cacti. The reality is slightly different.

Deserts are not named so because of their hot temperatures. They are called deserts because of a lack of water or moisture, and planet Earth has many cold deserts as well as hot ones. For example, the Atacama Desert in Chile is considered the driest place on Earth and is rather cold for a desert, with daily temperatures ranging from 32 to

77° F/0 to 25° C. Deserts are defined as areas with an average annual precipitation of less than 10 in./25 cm per year, or as areas where more water is lost by evaporation and transpiration (science-speak for the moisture given off by plants) than falls as rain.

LARGEST DESERTS

Below are the top ten largest deserts on Earth:

DESERT	CONTINENT	SIZE
Antarctic	Antarctica	5,400,000 mi² (14,000,000 km²)
Arctic	Arctic	5,427,000 mi² (14,056,000 km²)
Sahara	Africa	3,320,000 mi² (9,100,000 km²)
Arabian	Asia	900,000 mi² (2,330,000 km²)
Gobi	Asia	500,000 mi² (1,300,000 km²)
Kalahari	Africa	361,000 mi² (900,000 km²)
Patagonian	South America	253,000 mi² (650,000 km²)
Great Victoria	Australia	250,000 mi² (647,000 km²)
Syrian	Asia	200,000 mi² (520,000 km²)
Great Basin	North America	190,000 mi² (492,000 km²)

The deserts of the world occur on every continent including Antarctica, but most are found in the center or to the west of continents between 15 and 30 degrees north and south of the equator. The largest hot desert is the Sahara in northern Africa, covering more than 3 million mi^2/4 million km^2 and crossing twelve countries.

DESERT TYPES

Deserts are named and created in different ways, normally by where they are located and the main pattern of weather that occurs at that location. There are trade-wind deserts, mid-latitude deserts, deserts formed behind mountains, coastal deserts, high-altitude deserts and, of course, polar deserts.

Let's have a look at how they form.

Trade-Wind Deserts—The trade winds are found north and south of the equator. They pick up heat as they move back toward the equator. These dry winds remove moisture and cloud cover, which allows even more sunlight to heat the land. Most of the major deserts of the world lie in these areas. The world's largest desert, the Sahara of North Africa, has experienced seriously hot temperatures as high as 135° F/57° C. It is a trade-wind desert.

Rain Shadow Deserts—Rain shadow deserts are formed because tall mountain ranges prevent clouds filled with moisture from reaching areas on the far or protected side of mountain ranges. As hot air rises over the mountains, it condenses and produces rain, thus losing or using up its moisture content. The desert then forms in the rain "shadow" of the range because no moisture remains.

Coastal Deserts—Found mainly on the western sides of continents near the Tropics of Cancer and Capricorn. Coastal deserts are complex because they are created by interactions between the land, oceans and weather. A coastal desert, the Atacama of South America, is the Earth's driest desert. In the Atacama, measurable rainfall is less than .01 cm per year, but some places have not had rain for more than 400 years.

Mid-Latitude Deserts—These are found between 30 and 50 degrees north and south of the equator. These deserts are found near the center of continents and far away from oceans. They have a wide range of annual temperatures and can get very hot and also very cold. The Sonoran Desert, which borders the United States and Mexico, is a typical mid-latitude desert.

Montane Deserts—These are dry places with a very high altitude, such as several parts of the Himalayan mountain range. Many deserts within this category are higher than 10,000 ft./3,000 m. These places have an average annual precipitation of less than 1.5 in./4 cm and are normally very cold.

Polar Desert—Areas with annual precipitation less than 9.8 in./25 cm and a mean temperature during the warmest month of less than 50° F/10° C. Sand dunes are not the main features in these types of desert; ice and snow are the common occurrence.

SURVIVAL TIPS

Deserts are hostile and potentially deadly environments. If you find yourself in any type of desert, you will need to be well prepared.

1. In hot deserts, high temperatures can cause rapid loss of water due to sweating. A lack of sufficient water supplies or sources of water can lead to dehydration and hyperthermia. Hyperthermia can occur when the body cannot cool its core temperature and overheats. Watch out for some of the signs, which include headaches, dizziness, cramps, weakened breathing and a body temperature close to or above 104° F/40° C. If untreated, hyperthermia can result in death. To prevent this, your main priority is to cool down the patient and reduce body temperature. Apply a

cool cloth. Never use ice or very cold water as this could result in a thermal shock, which could kill. Keep the patient in a shaded, well-ventilated area and ensure that the cloth remains wet. When the temperature falls below 100° F/38° C, you can remove the cloth, but if the temperature begins to rise again, reapply it.

2. In cold deserts, hypothermia (the opposite of hyperthermia) and frostbite are the main problems, as well as dehydration. A lack of heat to melt the abundant ice means you are without a water supply.

3. Falling through ice layers into freezing water is a particular danger requiring emergency action to prevent rapid hypothermia, where the core body temperature drops rapidly. The patient will begin to shiver and become disorientated. In some cases, the person is so confused he may even begin to remove clothing, which only increases heat loss. To save the patient, you should shelter him away from sources of cold. Remove any wet clothing and begin rewarming the patient by giving additional clothing, hot drinks and additional heating, if possible.

DEADLY DESERT DWELLERS

If you manage to defy all of this, you have done well but are not out of the woods (or desert) yet. Planet Earth has some very well adapted beauties to unleash on you in the desert.

The Death Stalker or Palestinian Yellow Scorpion

This dweller grows to around 4.5 in./11.5 cm and appears very delicate compared to more heavily armored scorpions—but don't be fooled. The native of North

Africa and Middle East deserts has venom that packs a punch. While not powerful enough to kill a healthy human adult, the young, elderly or those with health problems are at greater risk. A single sting can trigger a life-threatening allergic reaction.

The Horned Desert Viper

This may appear to be quite cute with its distinctive horns at the front of its head but make no mistake—this guy is very well adapted to the desert environment and is also known as the sidewinder because of its movement across sand in a sideways fashion. Again, the venom of this creature is not deadly but it will set you back with vomiting, nausea, swollen limbs and even internal bleeding.

Inland Taipan

A native of Australia, this snake is actually quite shy but can be very aggressive if threatened. Its color varies depending on the season, and it can change from a rich brown to an olive green. On average, the taipan measures 6 ft./1.8 m in length. The AVRU (Australian Venom Research Unit) has ranked it as the most venomous snake on Earth, and before the development of an anti-venom in 1955, 90 percent of bites were said to be fatal in humans. Once bitten, the venom can potentially kill in forty-five minutes if anti-venom is not given.

Science Factoid

In hot deserts, temperatures can be so high that raindrops can often evaporate before they have the chance to hit the ground.

Massive Mass Movements

Fortunately, you now know that planet Earth is stronger than humans. This critical fact, mixed with your desire to conquer everything on the planet, puts you right in nature's firing line. So, paying close attention to this chapter could be the difference between you covering yourself in glory or covering yourself in snow, mud or rocks.

Take gravity, for instance. It may appear a very basic force that makes apples fall from trees, but it can generate some truly massive movements of soil, rock, water, ice and snow. Under the weight of gravity, materials can move rapidly downhill, and the deadly effects are greatly increased in high mountain areas so . . . beware!

The three main categories of mass movements are avalanches,

landslides and rock falls.

The frequency of these hazards is increasing due to population growth and pressure for space, forcing more people onto slopes and hillsides that could be unstable. This is especially true in poorer countries where huge developments of often illegal and poorly built towns seem to sprout up overnight.

AVALANCHES

Avalanches are the movement of snow and ice. They can move seriously fast. They are the most rapidly moving of all mass movements and are made up of snow but also rocks, ice and water. Several basic things must occur for an avalanche to happen:

- A hill or mountain has a slope of at least 25 degrees. Any less and the snow will not slide downhill.

- There is an increase in the weight of snow on steep slopes following a heavy snowfall or some spring rainfall.

- Snow tends to build up in layers just like a cake. A weaker layer can develop due to continuous thawing and re-freezing. This eventually destabilizes the built-up snowfield.

- All you need now is a trigger, which can be as large as an earthquake or as small as a skier.

Once an avalanche has been triggered, I'm afraid the statistics are not in your favor. Between 55 and 65 percent of people buried in the open during an avalanche are killed. This figure rises to 80 percent once the hour mark is reached.

The snow will start to slide at first but soon builds up enough speed to make the snow tumble. As the wave of snow builds speed, it can travel at speeds in excess of 60 mi./96 km per hour; however, some can travel even faster. "Powder snow" avalanches are the largest and most powerful, reaching speeds of 180 mi./289 km per hour. In large avalanches, the sheer volume of moving snow actually creates hurricane force winds that travel in front of the snow and have the power to rip roofs off houses and tear trees out of the ground.

SURVIVAL TIPS

1. Check out the forecasts for your area and see if any avalanches are expected there. If a warning is issued, listen to it and go home.

2. Luckily, the management of avalanches is improving all the time and some avalanches do give warnings. If this is the case, the threat can be reduced using snow fences to trap movement, planting trees and even using explosions to remove the threat . . . KABOOM!

3. Groups should spread out as they cross a mountain. This will improve the survival chances and should ensure that there are some people free to search for those trapped.

4. If you find yourself being carried by the snow in an avalanche, use a swimming motion. This may help keep you as close to the surface of the snow as possible, increasing your rescue chances.

5. Ditch as much equipment as possible. It will hold you down and hinder you from "swimming" at or near the surface of the snow.

6. As the avalanche begins to slow and stop, you should move your head from side to side and backward and forward. Then cover your mouth with one hand. This will help create a "breathe space" before the snow fully compacts. Similarly, you should take a deep breath at this point and hold it. This will allow for chest expansion.

TRIVIA   Angry Avalanches

- Records show that the feared warrior Hannibal lost around 18,000 men to avalanches in 218 BC as he crossed the alps to fight the Romans. It is also reported that he lost 2,000 horses and many elephants.

- In the Italian Alps between 1915 and 1918, it's estimated that 60,000 soldiers fighting in World War I lost their lives to avalanches. Troops often bombed snowfields above the enemy to create avalanches to use as weapons against them.

- In Ranrahirca, Peru, in 1962, a single avalanche killed nearly 4,000 people.

- On February 23, 1999, an avalanche destroyed the Austrian town of Galtür; 31 people were killed.

- On February 9, 1999, in the ski resort of Montroc near Chamonix, France, a large avalanche killed 12 people.

LANDSLIDES: SUPER SLOW OR SUPER WHOA?

Landslides are the movement of rock and soil.

Believe it or not, some mass movements are very slow affairs and aren't really that exciting. For example, soil creep does just that—it creeps at a rate of less than 1 cm and as such we are not going to focus on slow movements. Instead, we will concentrate on landslides, but even they can be classed from very slow to extremely rapid. These categories have speeds that vary from a snail's pace of 0.19 ft./ 0.06 m per year to a whooping 10 ft./3 m per second!

Some of the key ingredients that cause landslides are earthquakes and prolonged rainfall, which saturates (fills it up) soil and makes it heavier and more lubricated. The underlying rock beneath the soil or surface rocks is important because it acts like a slide itself. The rock type is also crucial, since broken rock is more likely to move than solid material.

Human activity doesn't help either. More houses, buildings and roads add more weight to the slopes. Combine this with digging and drilling for construction and slopes are made even more unstable. In some places, deforestation has left soils and rock exposed to the elements, which often causes dangerous mudflows.

TRIVIA

- Piave Valley, Italy, 1963. A huge rockslide slid into the reservoir and created a wave 230 ft./70 m high, which rose above the dam and down the valley where it destroyed the town of Longarone and killed around 2,000 people.

- In May 1970, a large earthquake shook parts of Peru and loosened a chunk of ice and snow near the top of the Huascaran Mountain. Ice and snow fell almost 10,000 ft./3,000 m and triggered an avalanche that was estimated to have hit the village of Yungay at 300 mi./480 km per hour. When rescuers eventually reached the town three days later, the town was buried beneath 100 ft./30 m of rock and debris and there were very few survivors from the town's 20,000 people.

- In northern Venezuela in 1999, a combination of very heavy rainfall and the exposed soils caused by deforestation led to a deadly combination of land and mudslides in which almost 30,000 people died and almost half a million people were made homeless.

SURVIVAL TIPS

1. Some slides have warning signs—look out for bulging walls, bowed fences and loud cracking noises.

2. Get away from low areas—gravity is the key here and rocks and mud slide downhill. If a landslide is on its way, get to the highest point in the area that is farthest away from the landslide.

3. If you are indoors, you are only safe in a structurally sound building. Lower floors can be swamped with debris. It's best to get as high as you can, as soon as you can.

4. Get a shield—if you are outdoors, you will need a large and strong shield. Your best hope is to position yourself behind a large building or in a structure like a cave.

5. Last options—If there are no buildings or structures in sight, then hide behind a large object to protect you from the flow. Any object that could redirect or obstruct the flow will be better to hide behind, such as a strong fence or large boulder.

ROCK FALLS

Rock falls are the movement of a single rock or groups of rocks.

Rock falls are classed as "on-going risks" because a rock or a bunch of them can be dislodged at any time. Thankfully, they are very rare and require very steep slopes with an angle of more than 40 degrees. Once a rock has broken off, it will either fall vertically or bounce to the foot of a slope, which is very difficult to plan for or avoid. Rock on!

Pyroclastic "Bombs"

Pyroclastic flows, which are mentioned earlier in the volcano chapter, are absolutely deadly! They are comprised of hot rock fragments, lava particles, ash and hot gases. Pyroclastic material can often be seen traveling as an ominous nuée ardente, which is French for "glowing cloud." These are spectacular and potentially lethal clouds traveling at speeds of 450 mi./724 km per hour and containing pyroclastic bombs as big as a house that are heated to 1,472° F/800° C. These have the capacity to blast, scorch and smother everything in their way!

PYROCLASTIC PERILS

- In 1902, on the Caribbean island of Martinique, the volcano of Mount Pelée erupted violently. The eruption created several nuée ardentes that rapidly swept down the sides of the mountain toward the main port, killing all but two of the town's 28,000 residents with heat and choking gases. Both survivors had severe burns to their bodies.

- Centuries after the eruption of Mount Vesuvius in southern Italy, which buried the town of Pompeii, scientists uncovered the town to find buried residents had covered their mouths to shield themselves from the gases and ash.

Plaster cast of Roman victim found at Pompeii.

- A pyroclastic flow from Mount Unzen, in Japan, in 1991 killed 43 people by engulfing them completely.

- Volcanic bombs are another hazard common to pyroclastic flows. These are heated rock fragments that are larger than 2.5 in./65 mm in diameter. These can cause severe injuries and death to people near an eruption zone. In 1993, an eruption of "bombs" at the Galeras volcano in Colombia killed six people near the volcano top and seriously injured several others.

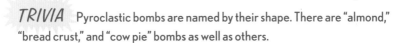

TRIVIA   Pyroclastic bombs are named by their shape. There are "almond," "bread crust," and "cow pie" bombs as well as others.

SURVIVAL TIPS

As with other volcanic hazards, make sure you've done your homework and compile a safety checklist:

1. Do your research—Is the volcano active at the moment? Is it due for an eruption soon? Do its eruptions normally produce pyroclastic flows?

2. Assess the terrain—These hazards flow down volcano sides "hugging" the ground and traveling to lower points. It is best to avoid areas of low sea level and valley floors.

3. Find safe haven—If you are in a tent, everything will be scorched and burned. Have a back-up plan such as a large cave or building to get deep inside. A wooden building is useless as it will be torched like any other flammable item. This still won't totally guarantee survival as toxic gases may enter your haven. One survivor of such an event claimed he held his breath while the toxic cloud passed by.

4. After the event—If you are fortunate enough to get through this, be careful. The few survivors of these events have often ventured outside too soon, resulting in badly burned feet as they pass over charred materials. Even your shoes will melt. It's best to wait a while until temperatures cool.

YOUNG SCIENTIST ACTIVITY
How to Make Your Own Volcanic Eruption

Also known as the "Cola and Mentos" eruption, this experiment is not only popular but massively successful in generating a huge bubbling eruption—so much so that it is best performed outdoors unless, of course, you want to cover mom's house in cola from ceiling to floor, which is not a good plan.

EQUIPMENT NEEDED:

1. A large bottle of cola (some say diet cola produces even better results)

2. Half a pack of Mentos mints

3. A kitchen funnel or tube (not essential but makes transfer of the Mentos into the cola much easier)

INSTRUCTIONS:

1. Again, it is best to make sure you are doing this experiment in a place where you won't get in trouble for getting cola everywhere. Outdoors is best.

2. Place your large cola bottle on a flat piece of ground or a stable surface like a board. Place it upright and unscrew the lid. If you have a funnel or tube, place it into the top of the bottle's neck. (This makes it easier to drop the Mentos into the cola.) Otherwise, this part of the experiment can become difficult and you may not be able to guide all the Mentos into the bottle.

3. Now, drop the Mentos into the cola and get clear! If done correctly, you should have created an enormous eruption of cola flying out of the bottle. It's a very impressive sight, with some experiments reaching about 30 ft./9 m high!

Science Factoid

Opinions about the exact science behind how this experiment works vary, but most people agree that it is the combination of CO_2 in the cola reacting vigorously with the little dimples found on Mentos candy pieces.

The thing that makes soda drinks bubbly is the CO_2 that is pumped into them at the factory. This gas doesn't get released from the liquid until you pour it into a glass and drink it. Some also gets released when you open the lid (more if you shake it up beforehand). This means that there is a whole lot of CO_2 gas just waiting to escape the liquid in the form of bubbles.

Dropping something into the diet cola speeds up this process by both breaking the surface tension of the liquid and also allowing bubbles to form on the surface area of the Mentos. Mentos candy pieces are covered in tiny dimples (a bit like a golf ball), which dramatically increases the surface area and allows a huge amount of bubbles to form around them. This combination of features means that when these two products are thrown together, there is an immediate release of a huge number of bubbles and a massive eruption.

Subterranean Surprises

WHAT DO WE MEAN BY SUBTERRANEAN?

The word "subterranean" comes from two words. "Sub" means below or underneath. "Terrain" means ground. Simply put them together and you've got underground. Some of the best exploration is found underground mainly because these areas are dark, secretive and largely undiscovered. Having said that, for thousands of years a good number of humans made their homes in caves. They not only provided shelter from the weather but they were a safe haven from an enemy attack. Where would cavemen have been without caves?

Speleology is the science of exploration and the study of all elements of caves and the environments that surround them.

HOW DO CAVES FORM?

Caves form in many ways—some are found in cliffs at the coast and have been chipped away by pounding waves. Others form where a lava tube's outer surface cools and hardens and the inside of the molten rock drains away. Caves can even form in glaciers where the meltwater carves tunnels at the beginning of its journey to the sea.

Most underground caves, however, form in karst—a type of landscape made of limestone, dolomite and gypsum rocks that slowly dissolves due to water that is slightly acidic.

Rain + CO_2 = dissolved rock

The rain mixes with CO_2 in the atmosphere as it falls to the ground and then picks up more of the gas as it seeps into the soil. The combination is a weak acid that can dissolve calcite, which is the main mineral of karst rocks.

The acidic water percolates down into the Earth through cracks and fractures and creates a network of passages like a giant underground plumbing system. The passages widen as more water seeps down, allowing even more water to flow through them. Eventually, some of the passages become large enough to earn the distinction of becoming a cave, but this doesn't happen overnight. These features can take more than 100,000 years to widen large enough to hold a single human being.

This process is similar to that of acid rain, which erodes and badly disfigures limestone buildings, monuments and statues.

STRANGE FEATURES

Hidden in the darkness of caves are all manner of rock formations!

The icicle-shaped formations are called stalactites and form as water drips from the cave roof. Stalagmites grow up from the floor, usually from the water that drips off the end of stalactites. Columns form where stalactites and stalagmites join. Sheets of calcite growths on cave walls and floors are called flowstones. Other stalactites take the form of draperies and soda straws. Twisty shapes called helictites warp in all directions from the ceiling, walls and floor.

Stalactite
Stalagmite

People often have difficulties remembering the difference between stalagmites and stalactites, but there is an old rhyme that might help you:

"When the tights (tites) go down, the mites go up."

CRAZY CAVE DWELLERS!

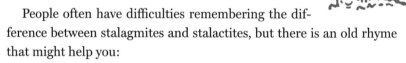

Many cave species have evolved very differently to those on the surface. Many are blind because of the lack of light. Most permanent cave dwellers lack any color in their skin because they have no pigment. Recently, many new animal species were discovered in a cave near Israel, including freshwater and saltwater creatures living in the same cave.

You must not confuse your cave-dwelling creatures! Troglobites are species that live in caves all the time, whereas troglophiles are species that can live their entire lives in caves but also occur in other environments. There are also trogloxenes, which are species that use caves but cannot complete their life cycle wholly housed away in a cave.

WATCH YOUR STEP, BOY!

If you are even walking on the surface of a karst limestone pavement, you must be very careful. Even if you defy the clints and grikes (the deep gashes and blocks that lie on karst surfaces) without getting a twisted ankle, you need to be wary of much greater risks such as vanishing streams and swallow holes. These are, of course, surface streams that literally disappear through gaps in the rock, and they do so by creating huge openings called swallow holes. These may be in the roof of huge caverns, and you really don't want to drop down one of these. In Yorkshire, England, there is a swallow hole christened "Gaping Gill" that has a 110-m drop. That's more than 360 ft. down!

In the past, people have foolishly built on karst limestone. Caverns often form beneath the surface and are not detected until it is too late. In Florida in 1981, a house and six cars fell into an undetected cavern when the roof of the cavern caved in. The hole left was more than 650 ft./198 m wide (about the length of two football fields) and more than 160 ft./48 m deep (that's almost the height of the Horseshoe Falls at Niagara).

TRIVIA Agartha is a legendary city that is said to reside in the Earth's core. It is related to the belief in a hollow Earth that is accessible to people. Much has been written about Agartha and the city is a key teaching in Buddhism. There are differing ideas about where this society is located, but many stories place it in central Asia, north of Tibet, and only those who are truly pure in spirit will be granted entrance to it.

Dixia Cheng, the underground city in Beijing, is a relic of the Chinese-Soviet border conflict in 1969—a time when Chairman Mao ordered the construction of subterranean bomb shelters in case of nuclear attack. The tunnels, which were built from 1969 to 1979, cover more than 18 mi./29 km and are found 26–60 ft./8–18 m under the surface. This impressive construction includes nearly a thousand anti-air raid structures.

Subterranean dwellers would not have died of boredom either. Classrooms were constructed for children, who lived in the underground city, and amenities like those found aboveground—like movie theaters, barbershops and restaurants—were found.

YOUNG SCIENTIST ACTIVITY
The dissolvable eggshell

This experiment needs time and a lot of patience but the science behind it is really cool.

EQUIPMENT NEEDED:

A container or beaker

One raw egg

Vinegar

INSTRUCTIONS:

1. Place your egg into the container or beaker.

2. Cover the egg completely with the vinegar.

3. Now comes the hard part—leave the egg for one whole week.

4. Return to your egg and lift it out. What do you notice?

Science Factoid

The vinegar is an acid and it reacts with the eggshell, which is made from calcium carbonate. The vinegar breaks the eggshell into its separate calcium and carbonate parts, literally dissolving the shell.

Petrifying Poles

You may have heard the old saying "We're poles apart," meaning two people couldn't be any farther apart if they tried. The North and South Poles work in exactly the same way. Yes, of course, one is on top of the planet and one is on the bottom, but if you take a closer look there is so much more that sets the North and South Poles apart from each other.

The North Pole, or the Arctic, is a frozen ocean surrounded by continents while the South Pole, or Antarctic, is a frozen continent surrounded by ocean. Even the names of the poles are opposite—the Ancient Greeks knew Antarctica was there despite never having seen it. They simply believed it had to be there to balance the North Pole.

They called it "Anti-Arkitos," or "opposite."

If you needed any further proof of these polar opposites, just look at their reversed seasons—due to tilt of the Earth's axis, it is summertime in the Arctic and winter in Antarctica, and vice versa.

HONEY, I'VE JUST HAD A REAAAALLLLLLYYYY LONG DAY!

At the North and South Poles, a day can last up to six months and a night can be just as long. This happens because the Earth's axis tilts at an angle of a little under 23.5 degrees. As it spins, the top of the axis points at the sun for six months and then away. That means that at the extreme north and south, the poles may have the sun in the sky for six months without setting, or, in winter, six months without a sunrise. Farther out near the Arctic and Antarctic circles, places are not affected as much and may only experience a single day of complete sunlight or darkness.

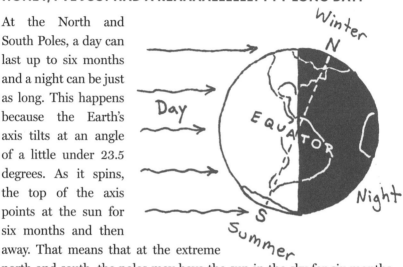

THE ICE CAPS: EARTH'S VERY OWN SUNGLASSES

Strange as it may sound, the ice caps at the top and bottom of the planet with their freezing temperatures help keep the human race at just the right temperature to be livable—this is part of nature's clever cooling system.

At the equator, the sun is directly overhead and that's why it receives the most sunlight. At the poles, the overhead sun is at a much lower angle and the energy received is low. This is because energy has much more atmosphere to pass through at the poles so more is lost or scattered or reflected.

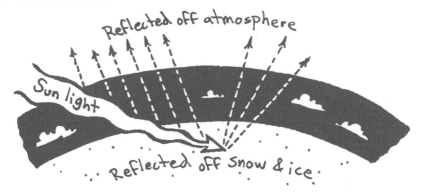

On top of that, the poles are a design masterpiece—they are colored white for a reason and maximize their albedo. What did you say? The term "albedo" (pronounced "al-bee-doh") is scientists' way of describing how reflective the different surfaces on planet Earth are.

Earth's oceans and dark-colored soils are not good at reflecting the sun and have a very low albedo, only about 10 percent. Fresh snow is quite the opposite and has a high albedo or reflectivity, around 85 percent or more. This means that the North and South Poles act like giant mirrors or sunglasses that reflect most of the sunlight they receive back into the atmosphere and help keep us at just the right temperature.

NORTH POLE FACTOIDS

- Over half the Arctic Ocean is covered in sea ice that is 10 ft./3 m thick.

- Many explorers and scientists believed the Arctic was like Antarctica and was a thick layer of ice on a vast continent, but in 1958 submariners (people who use submarines) sailed right under the ice cap and came out the other side.

- The North Pole has a latitude of 90 degrees and a longitude of 0 degrees.

- Classed as "the warm pole," the Arctic summer temperatures can rise well above freezing while winter days can average -86° F/-30° C.

SOUTH POLE FACTOIDS

- Antarctica is roughly one and a half times the size of Europe and around sixty times bigger than the U.K. (Don't get lost!)

- The continent of Antarctica is the only continent on Earth with no "indigenous" people—fancy-speak for "locals." There are a few thousand research scientists who have set up bases to study the continent, but no one really goes there to live.

- It is the coldest, windiest, highest and driest continent on Earth—Antarctica is technically a frozen desert.

- If all Antarctic ice were to melt, the sea level would rise almost 200 ft./60 m.

- The coldest temperature recorded at any place on Earth was the Vostok Station, Antarctica, in July 1983. The temperature fell to -192° F/-89° C.

POLAR TOUGH GUYS

You need to be extremely tough and really well adapted to defy the polar regions. Let's take one contender from each of the icy poles and see who is the toughest. Representing the Arctic is the polar bear. The Antarctic tough cookie is the emperor penguin.

The polar bear is the largest land carnivore on Earth. An adult male can measure 10 ft./3 m and weigh around 770–1,500 lbs./350–680 kg. Polar bears are amazingly adapted to defy cold temperatures as well as move across snow, ice and open water. Their coats appear ivory or snow-white in color, allowing all visible light to be reflected while their outer hairs, or "guard hairs," are actually clear and hollow. This fabulous design means that a polar bear's coat releases almost no heat—so much so that the bear can't even be seen by infrared camera! The polar bear is an accomplished swimmer and can swim up to 50 mi./80 km without resting. This is aided by a 4-in./10-cm layer of fat beneath the skin that not only insulates but gives buoyancy to aid in swimming. In winter, polar bears must endure average temperatures of -86° F/-30° C and also find food to stay alive. They will travel across areas of more than 150 mi./241 km to track seals for survival, which is much farther than any other species of bear.

The emperor is the tallest and heaviest of all penguin species and can grow to 4 ft./1.2 m in height and weigh anything from 48–99 lbs./22–45 kg. They are the only penguin species that breed during the Antarctic winter. Every other animal species leave the continent at this time. The males, who care for the eggs until they hatch, endure the worst winter conditions on Earth. They face temperatures of -158° F/-70° C, fierce winds, and four months with no sunlight, food, or water. Firstly, the penguin treks 31–75 mi./50–120 km over the ice to breeding colonies that may include thousands of individuals. The female lays a single egg, which is incubated by the male while the female returns to the sea to feed. The dedicated dads huddle in packs and take turns rotating from the exposed edges of the huddle to the warm center. Now, who do you think is the toughest polar inhabitant?

ATTACK OF THE POLAR ZOMBIES

Many early explorers to both the Arctic and Antarctica suffered with a terrible disease known as "scurvy," until 1800 when cures for it started to spread. The deficiency disease is caused by a lack of vitamin C. We can only gain vitamin C from certain foods such as vegetables, fruits and raw meats (cooking starts to breakdown the vitamin C content). Many early sailors and polar explorers suffered from this disease because food supplies on long journeys would lose their vitamin C content after a while. The effects of scurvy can be gross unless you're into looking and smelling like a foul-breathed, open sore–wearing zombie!

Scurvy makes the small blood vessels in your body weaken and old cuts or wounds can begin to re-open. Bruises start to become widespread across the body, while bleeding gums and loosening teeth are common. After that, bleeding into muscles and joints increases the amount of pain you feel and disorientation makes you feel like you're going crazy. If untreated, explorers could die from heart or breathing difficulties.

In the worst cases reported, sufferers were described as looking like bloated yellow carcasses with green, red and yellow blotches caused by bleeding at different stages. Ulcers develop and sores on skin open and weep with an awful smell—nice!

SURVIVAL TIPS

1. Have the right equipment—You will need the following as a bare minimum: lots of loose, warm clothing (loose clothing is essential to help the circulation of body heat and sweat evaporation), backpack, weather-proof jacket, skis or snowshoes, goggles or sunglasses (to avoid snow blindness), sunscreen, polar balaclava, snow gloves, a flare (if in danger), a sleeping bag, a tent, a small shovel, fire-starting equipment, cooking equipment, a compass, a map, a knife and plenty of food.

2. Time your visit accurately—The Arctic in summer can lose most of its ice and can be very hazardous to explore at this time. It is better to wait for sufficient ice cover. Equally, it is not advisable to explore Antarctica during its winter (Northern Hemisphere summer) as temperatures can regularly be below -122°F/-50° C. Research the weather closely to find the best time to visit each pole.

3. Stay dry—Getting wet in polar regions can spell disaster for an explorer and expose you to all sorts of difficulties including frostbite.

4. A place to shelter—All the issues mentioned so far are important, but if temperatures drop too far and winds pick up to hurricane force, then your tent is going to struggle to protect you. Your best option is to dig a snow hole:

- Use the small shovel—You will need a sheltered area. Ideally, your hideout will back onto a rock face that will give some shelter from wind and snow, but with a deep enough supply of snow for you to burrow into.

- Check the consistency of the snow—It can't be too powdery. It must have sufficient moisture to hold its shape.

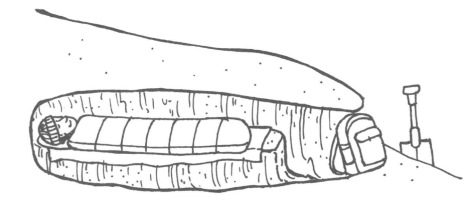

- Check the wind—Make sure the wind is not blowing directly into your snow hole. It will be too cold if it is.

- Make a hole—Dig a hole that is wide enough to allow you through it. Dig for about 8 ft./2 m or so and then start to widen out the hole into a living space that will be large enough for you to lie down in.

- Build a bed—Once your chamber starts to take shape, you will need to build a "bed" out of the snow. This will be a raised area of snow (a bit like a bench). This is essential for your comfort as cold air sinks to the floor and warm air rises. Your raised "bed" will be warmer.

- Lock the door—Get all your equipment inside and use your backpack to seal off the door.

- Stay dry—Place any waterproof materials on top of your "bed" and place your sleeping bag on top of them. (This will keep you and your sleeping bag from getting wet.)

5. Energy levels—High energy levels are essential at the poles. Eat and drink regularly, and get plenty of rest at night.

GETTING ALONG WITH THE LOCALS

The only people you will run into in Antarctica are other explorers or some scientists. However, at the North Pole there are numerous cultures including the Sami and the Inuit peoples. The native groups of the Arctic speak many different languages and many more different dialects, but here are a few Inuit or Inuktitut sayings that should help you if you are in a bit of a fix:

ENGLISH	PRONUNCIATION IN INUKTITUT
Welcome	Toong-a-su-GIT
How are you?	Ka-nui-PIT?
I am cold.	Ik-KIIK-too-nga
I am hungry.	KAAK-too-nga
What is your name?	Ki-now-VIT?
Thank you	Koo-YAAN-na-miik
Can I use the bathroom?	a-NAR-vik a-too-roon-NAK-pa-ra?
Goodbye	TUG-vow-voo-tiit

Some "k" sounds are actually pronounced as "q."

Extraordinary Earthquakes

Earthquakes, like volcanoes, are usually found along plate margins and are caused by a huge buildup of pressure that happens as these mammoth plates are forced into one another. This enormous pressure is only released as rock in the plates gives way. The point at which an earthquake actually begins is deep below the Earth's surface and is called the focus. A deep focus is good because the effects of the earthquake may be less as the shockwaves have much more rock to move through. The point directly above the focus on the Earth's surface is called the epicenter. The effects of the earthquake are normally worst here.

HOW DEEP, HOW DAMAGING?

• Shallow focus earthquakes are found at depths between 0 and 43 mi./0 and 70 km. These are the most dangerous and account for 75 percent of all earthquakes worldwide.

• Intermediate focus earthquakes are found between 44 and 186 mi./70–300 km deep.

• Deep focus earthquakes are found as a deep as 187–435 mi./300–700 km down. These do the least damage.

HOW DO THE WAVES WORK?

Seismic waves radiate out from the focus beneath the ground, just as the ripples on a pond do when you throw a stone in to it! There are three types of seismic waves, which travel at different speeds:

Primary—or P waves, are speedy seismic waves that travel fastest and vibrate in the direction they travel. You will feel these first. They reach speeds of 3.4 mi./5.5 km per second, which is eight times faster than the Concorde, the fastest airliner ever built.

Secondary—or S waves, are only half as fast as P waves, but they can really make rocks shake. By traveling at right angles to the rock, these guys can make concrete and buildings shake like pieces of ribbon in the wind.

Surface—These waves take a longer route along the Earth's surface and are the last to arrive, but when they do, they are sure to announce themselves. They cause the Earth to roll like the top of the ocean. These are the guys that make bridges sway to and fro, and cause power cables and gas pipes to snap. Some seismologists (earthquake specialists) describe the slow surface waves as the "sting" in the earthquake's tail!

ENORMOUS EARTHQUAKES OVER THE PAST 100 YEARS

YEAR	COUNTRY	DEATHS	MAGNITUDE ON RICHTER SCALE	COST IN U.S. DOLLARS
1908	Messina, Italy	Approx. 26,000	7.5	116 million
1920	Gansu, China	235,000	8.6	25 million
1923	Tokyo, Japan	143,000	8.3	2.8 million
1976	Tangshan, China	Approx. 300,000	8.0	5.6 million
1990	Western Iran	Approx. 50,000	7.7	Unknown
2001	India	Approx. 100,000	7.7	1.8 million

EARTHQUAKE EFFECTS

The effects of earthquakes, like volcanoes, can be split into the primary and secondary effects. Primary effects are those that occur immediately as the earthquake is happening. These can be deadly and result in buildings collapsing and roads and bridges being destroyed, which are caused by the violent shaking of the ground. Falling buildings or debris kills many people instantly.

Secondary effects are the later effects of the quake, and can be even more devastating than the primary ones. The main secondary effects include:

Fires—Fires can break out anywhere and are usually caused by damaged electrical equipment and burst gas pipes. This was the main cause of death and damage after the San Francisco earthquake of 1906.

Tsunami—A giant wave caused by an earthquake is called a tsunami. They can travel very quickly across entire oceans, before engulfing land thousands of miles away. The 1964 Alaskan earthquake caused considerable damage in several Californian coastal areas. Although Los Angeles has escaped so far, it is still classed as a tsunami-prone area.

Landslides and avalanches—These are often triggered by earthquakes, causing huge amounts of rock, soil, snow, ice or water to be moved very quickly. This is what occurred just before the volcanic eruption of Mount St. Helens. They are most likely to occur where the land is steep and has been weakened in some way.

Diseases—Diseases can spread very quickly due to unsanitary conditions often left behind by massive earthquakes. Waterborne diseases such as typhoid and cholera spread easily. Poorer nations are especially at risk where access to medical services can be badly hampered by the damage caused by the quake.

MEASURING AN EARTHQUAKE

There are two separate scales for measuring earthquakes:

1. The Richter (pronounced "Rick-ter") scale measures the magnitude (geography word for strength) of an earthquake using an instrument called a seismograph. The Richter scale is a logarithmic scale. That means that an earthquake measuring 8 produces 10 times more shaking than one measuring 7, and 100 times more shaking than one measuring 6. The energy

levels released are also linked, but for each unit increase on the scale, the energy released increases by 30 times. In other words, an earthquake measuring 4 on the Richter scale is 30 times more powerful than one measuring 3 on the scale.

2. The Mercalli scale doesn't measure the actual size of the earthquake itself but the damage it does. It ranks each earthquake from 1 to 12 (the scale is actually written in Roman numerals, so 1–12 looks like I–XII), depending on how much damage was done. A quake that causes a lightbulb to sway measures III on the Mercalli scale while XII signals total devastation.

SURVIVAL TIPS

1. Before the earthquake, prepare a survival kit with water, food, blankets, first-aid kit, flashlight and radio.

2. If you are indoors during an earthquake, make sure you are away from any objects that can fall on you and injure you.

3. Crawl beneath a strong piece of furniture like a kitchen table or a desk and stay there until the quake is over.

4. Keep away from items that can shatter, such as windows and mirrors. These can badly injure you.

5. If caught outdoors, stay away from any object that can fall on you. These include trees, buildings and power lines. Try to find an area of open space where you will be safest.

6. After a quake, you still need to be alert. Aftershocks (smaller quakes after the main event) can still cause damage. Rubble can be dangerous to get across and the ground itself could have split. Not to mention the possibility of fires, gas explosions and the other hazards mentioned earlier.

YOUNG SCIENTIST ACTIVITY
Playing with Pressure

Pressure is an invisible but powerful force that drives our weather, results in earthquakes and makes the bottoms of our oceans such a mystery. Using this cool experiment, you can discover just how pressure works in the world around us.

EQUIPMENT NEEDED:

An empty aluminum soda can • One pair of kitchen tongs

One large saucepan • Cold water

INSTRUCTIONS:

1. Fill the saucepan with cold water.

2. Put a tablespoon of water inside the can.

3. Heat the can on the stove to boil the water inside.

4. When the water is boiled, a little cloud of condensation will rise out of the top of the can.

5. Quickly and carefully, use the tongs to lift the very hot can. Turn it completely upside down and place it in the saucepan of cold water.

6. Watch as the can is crushed immediately.

Science Factoid

Heating the can caused the water inside to boil. The water vapor from the boiling water forced the air inside of the can out. Once the can was filled with water vapor and then suddenly cooled, it caused the water vapor in the can to condense and created a vacuum. This vacuum inside the can made it easy for the pressure of the air outside the can to simply crush it.

Liquifying Earth

During some earthquakes, a strange phenomenon can take place where the land beneath your feet acts more like a liquid than a solid. Soil liquefaction happens when a soil containing a lot of water loses its binding qualities when shaken violently and starts to behave like a liquid. It is a similar feeling to standing on wet sand and wiggling your toes so that you begin to sink into it. The ground beneath you can behave like wibbly, wobbly Jell-O.

SURVIVAL TIPS

As with earthquakes themselves, there are many hazards associated with liquefaction, including fires, gas explosions and building collapse.

1. If you are in a city or any developed area, one of the biggest threats may be building collapse or subsidence. This can happen because the land the buildings are standing on simply starts to act like a liquid and the buildings fall over. If you are inside, try to find a large piece of furniture like a table and sit beneath it until the danger passes.

2. If you are outdoors, it is best to be away from buildings, power lines and trees as these can collapse when the ground liquefies and fall on top of you.

3. Lastly, stay calm. Those who panic usually run into problems that can be deadly. Yes, the ground beneath you will feel really weird but it won't last for long, and if you have found a safe place, you will most likely be ok. Also, places with high soil water content actually "dampen" the effect of the earthquake itself, thereby, making it less dangerous!

YOUNG SCIENTIST ACTIVITY
Turn Bone to Rubber

Here you will be able to turn a strong and sturdy chicken bone into a rubberized one, which bends and moves very easily.

EQUIPMENT NEEDED:

A container or beaker

One uncooked chicken bone

Vinegar

INSTRUCTIONS:

1. Clean and dry the chicken bone. It is best to leave it to dry overnight.

2. Place the bone in the container.

3. Take the vinegar and fill the container until the bone is completely covered.

4. Leave the bone in the solution for 6–7 days. What do you find?

Science Factoid

The acid in the vinegar works to dissolve the calcium in the chicken bone. The calcium is what makes bones strong; once this has been dissolved away, all that is left is a soft, flexible material that is bendable.

Weather Phenomena

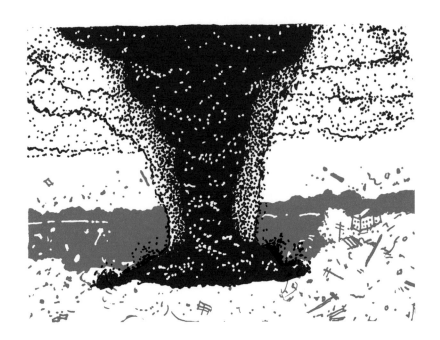

Tornadoes

Experts think that the word "tornado" is taken from the Spanish word "tronada," meaning thunderstorm, but tornadoes are much deadlier than any ordinary thunderstorm. These are nature's assassins and are the most violent of all atmospheric storms. Tornadoes are on a much smaller scale when compared with hurricanes and they have a much shorter lifespan, but this simply concentrates their enormous energy.

HOW DO TORNADOES FORM?

Tornadoes start out life quite beautifully with an elegant dance between bodies of warm and cold air. They start to form in huge thunderstorms called "super cells," which are driven by currents of warm, rising air. These strong and warm updrafts can begin to spin because of a deflective force called Coriolis force. If the spin is strong enough, then a vortex is created. Worse still, a funnel of air may appear below the storm cloud, and, if this touches the ground, a tornado is now in action. It will travel in the direction of the thunderstorm.

TORNADO ALLEY AND OTHER VICTIMS

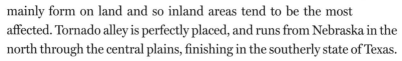

Tornado alley is a belt of land in the United States that experiences more tornadoes than anywhere else in the world. It also experiences more violent tornadoes than anywhere else. Unlike hurricanes, tornadoes mainly form on land and so inland areas tend to be the most affected. Tornado alley is perfectly placed, and runs from Nebraska in the north through the central plains, finishing in the southerly state of Texas.

Over 75 percent of all the recorded tornadoes in the world are recorded in the United States. The reason for this is, quite simply, because of its geography—central continental states are warmed in early spring and summer and these areas radiate heat back into the air, further warming the air, which is coming from the Gulf of Mexico. This air then meets cold air that has traveled from the Arctic, down through Canada and into the United States, and then the dance begins.

Other areas of Earth can be affected by tornadoes, but to a lesser degree. They can be found anywhere in the mid-latitudes, which is roughly the halfway point between the equator and the poles. The United Kingdom is located in the mid-latitudes and in any given year can have up to sixty tornadoes—watch out!

TORNADO DAMAGE SCALE

Tornadoes are measured using the F-Scale. This scale has six categories, which start out at F0 and work all the way up to F5. Look at the table below to see the damage.

F-SCALE CATEGORY	WIND SPEEDS	TYPE OF DAMAGE
F0	40–72 mph 64–115 km/h	Little damage is done with some tree branches broken.
F1	73–112 mph 117–180 km/h	Some damage to roof tiles and mobile homes may move.
F2	113–157 mph 182–252 km/h	More serious damage with roofs torn off houses.
F3	158–206 mph 254–331 km/h	Severe damage with forests flattened.
F4	207–260 mph 333–418 km/h	Devastation—few walls will remain standing with large-debris missiles thrown great distances.
F5	261–318 mph 420–511 km/h	Incredible damage—This rare tornado results in houses being leveled and debris removed. Top stories on larger buildings can be removed completely.

TORNADO TRIVIA

• There are many cases of houses being lifted off the ground, turned 360 degrees, and promptly plopped back down to Earth.

- On the 3rd of May 1999, over sixty tornadoes terrorized Kansas and Oklahoma, causing more than $1 billion in damage, forty-four deaths and almost 1,000 injuries.

- Tornadoes can appear nearly transparent until dust and debris are picked up.

- On the 18th of March 1925, the Great Tri-State Tornado started in Missouri, moved through Illinois and passed into Indiana. In total, there were 695 deaths and more than 2,000 people were injured.

TORNADO VARIATIONS

Tornadoes vary greatly and not just in size and strength. They can have their very own color depending on the debris being whipped around inside them. Others generate their own smell as lightning in the storm creates a sulfuric "rotten egg" smell.

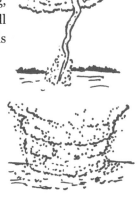

Waterspouts—These are tornadoes that have developed over a water source. Despite the name and even appearance that it is made of water, most of it is actually a cloud. That said, the amount of spray they can whip up could be deadly and there have been many deaths caused by these water funnels.

Spaghetti or Rope Tornadoes—These are long, wispy and often difficult to track. They are well named because they appear to look like giant strands of spaghetti or long, thin ropes.

Wide or Wedge Tornadoes—The wider a tornado is at its base, the more destructive it can be. Very wide tornadoes can generate winds of 250 mi./400 km per hour because air actually accelerates as it is drawn into a tornado. The greater the room within a tornado for air to accelerate, the faster it will get.

SURVIVAL TIPS

1. Weather experts estimate the average warning time for a tornado alert is about 13 minutes. You can look out for tornado telltale signs by looking for a dark, greenish sky, large hailstorms and a powerful, train-like roar.

2. If indoors, it is best to get as low as possible. Take refuge in a basement or the lowest floor of your home. Cover yourself with something soft like a mattress or hide under a table. Stay there.

3. If outdoors, look for a ditch or dip in the ground. Again, get as close to the ground as you can. Crouch up so that your knees are tight into your chest. Do this by wrapping your arms around your knees. Try to cover your head with something soft.

YOUNG SCIENTIST ACTIVITY
How to Build an Airship

Air and pressure are two of the key ingredients in the formation of a tornado. Using air and pressure, plus a few simple instruments, you can build your very own airship.

EQUIPMENT NEEDED:

A length of long string (about 20 ft./6.1 m long)

A straw

Some sticky tape

One balloon

A friend to help

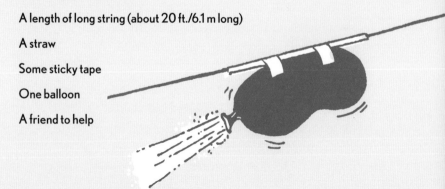

INSTRUCTIONS:

1. Get your friend to take one end of the string and attach it to something like a tree or fence.

2. Run the other end of the string through the straw and tie the end to another object so the string is nice and tight.

3. Now inflate the balloon but don't tie it (the air needs to escape for your airship to work).

4. Hold the end of the balloon and get your friend to tape the straw to the side of the balloon.

5. When you're ready. Let the balloon go . . . whizzzzzzz!!!!!

Science Factoid

This activity shows how air pressure can create winds. Winds are caused as air "rushes" from places of high pressure to areas of low pressure. The air inside the balloon is under greater pressure than the air outside the balloon. As you let go of the balloon, the air inside is forced out very quickly and this creates a thrust that forces your airship forward.

TRIVIA   The invisible air pressure all around us controls much of our weather. In the formation of a tornado, warm air rises under less pressure whereas cold air falls under greater pressure. This results in a kind of "dance" between the two, which soon speeds up!

Animal Rain

When we think of rain, most of us think of droplets of water falling from the skies to water our plants and fill our streams. However, sometimes rain can get a little crazy.

There is an old saying: "It's raining cats and dogs out there," and it could be closer to the truth than you might think. Animal rain is not as uncommon as it might sound. In fact, reports of such events occur quite regularly and from across the planet.

Other than rain itself, fish are the most common thing reported falling from the sky, but frogs, squid and other animals have been known to fall too.

HOW DO THEY GET UP THERE?

Scientists believe that animal rain is caused by strong updrafts of air passing over a piece of land or body of water that literally "suck" the animals into the air. These updrafts are most likely to occur where strong winds are present, such those as found in a thunderstorm or tornado.

Once picked up, the animals can be carried for several miles, but on some occasions animals have been taken hundreds of miles from where they first lifted off. Then, just like in normal rain, the clouds open and the fish, frogs and even turtles fall along with the rain.

IT'S RAINING WHAT?

- In 1864, a farmer in Quebec, Canada, found a frog perfectly preserved inside a large hailstone.

- In 1930, an 8-in./20-cm turtle fell from the skies during a storm in Mississippi (maybe it was a ninja turtle!).

- In 1976, Olympic yacht crew members reported that they were pelted by live maggots while sailing through a storm.

- In 1996, in the Welsh town of Llanddewi Brefi, people reported outbreaks of frog rain, and two years later a similar event was recorded in Croydon, South London.

THINGS TO DO

- Watch out—Look for large storm clouds gathering. The larger and darker the clouds, the greater the likelihood of a bigger storm. Also, look out for winds picking up and the very obvious "spout" or funnel of a tornado.

- Take cover—Animal rain might be cool to watch from inside a barn or house, but unless you want a head full of maggots or worms, it's best to get indoors. Which brings us to the next hazard—animal size. This has an influence on what type of injury is caused. Smaller animals, although disgusting, are not really going to cause you injury, but larger creatures falling from the sky just might. Imagine how painful it would be to get cracked over the head with the hard shell of a turtle or a hailstone so big it contained a frog inside? If you

are outdoors and can't get to shelter, look for some natural objects like a tree or a cave to get out of the way. A tree may not stop the object entirely, but it will slow it down as it bounces off the branches above your head (which should also be covered with your hands for extra protection)!

• Finally, record and report the event to your local weather center. You may also have found yourself a new family pet.

YOUNG SCIENTIST ACTIVITY
Playing with Gravity

In this experiment, the science is important but your skill is the key to its success. It may take a little practice to make sure you defy gravity, but over time you will get better at playing with the forces of nature. Things normally fall from the sky, like weird animal rain, but here you can play around and reverse normal patterns.

EQUIPMENT NEEDED:

One hair dryer

One Ping-Pong ball (as you become more expert, you can work up to more!)

INSTRUCTIONS:

1. Take the hair dryer and plug it into the electricity supply. Now turn it on the highest setting.

2. Hold the hair dryer so that it is pointing straight up in the air.

3. Set your Ping-Pong ball directly above the current of hot air coming out of the hair dryer. What happens?

Science Factoid

What you're actually doing here is playing with one of the forces of nature! The hot air from the hair dryer pushes the Ping-Pong ball up with a force that equals the force of gravity. Also, air pressure creates a column of air that the Ping-Pong ball is held inside, making it easier to control the movement of the ball. The tougher test is to control 2, 3 or even more Ping-Pong balls all at once. Having mastered this skill, you can draw a different animal onto each ball. You are now re-creating nature's warm updrafts—the strong currents responsible for lifting animals off the ground and up into the skies.

Dust Storms

Dust storms, aka sandstorms, can be one of the deadliest and most unpredictable hazards the Earth can throw at you. This is due to the fact that high winds, combined with large areas of sand, can make for a lethal cocktail that can disorientate its victims and even suffocate them. So, if you are feeling brave enough to tackle dust storms head on, then this chapter could be the difference between success and failure.

FACTS ABOUT DUST STORMS

- Dust storms are not just found on Earth. They are a regular occurrence on Mars.

- Although typically about 50 ft./15 m high, the "wall" of sand in a dust storm can be up to a 1 mi./1.6 km high.

- Deserts such as the Sahara and Gobi regions are common areas for dust storms, but they can also occur in any arid or semi-arid climate.

- Dust storms can move extremely quickly, traveling at speeds of up to 75 mi./120 km per hour—it's unlikely that you will outrun one on foot.

SURVIVAL TIPS

If a dust storm is already upon you, it is already too late to try and escape. Once cloaked by a storm, you will lose all sense of direction as visibility drops dramatically, sunlight is blocked out, and the sand begins to whip at your bare skin and eyes. Worse still, if you are unable to cover your mouth properly, sand will begin to enter your throat and lungs, which can be fatal. This is scary stuff, but with a few survival tips you will leave this planetary hazard fairly unscathed.

1. Preparation is critical—In a semi-desert or desert environment, you must expect dust storms to come with the territory. You must carry:

- A mask—Use this to cover your mouth and nose and to prevent suffocation.

- Airtight goggles—These can protect your eyes from serious damage. If you aren't prepared with either of the above, use a piece of clothing to cover the eyes, mouth and nose.

- Protective clothing—Ideally, these should be wind-proof materials that will prevent you from being sanded away to nothing.

2. Drive away—If you are in a vehicle and you see a storm in the distance, try to avoid it by driving away.

3. Batten down the hatches—If you are indoors, make sure all windows and doors are shut and just wait. If you are in a vehicle, pull over and wait.

4. Find higher ground or park your camel—If you are unlucky enough to be outdoors, try to get to higher ground. The heaviest and densest material is nearest ground level. It is best to move to where the dust is finer and less intense. Failing that, if you happen to be on a camel, park it fast, and sit behind it. The camel's body will give you shelter from the worst of the storm.

Horrid Hurricanes

C an you tell the difference between a typhoon and a willy-willy? Do you know what sets a hurricane apart from a cyclone? Well, all four of the above—a typhoon, a willy-willy, a hurricane and a cyclone—are classed as "tropical storms." In fact, they are all exactly the same hazard, but their names simply show where on Earth they are experienced. In Australia, they call their tropical storms "willy-willies." In Pacific Asia, they are called "typhoons." Storms coming off the Indian Ocean are called "cyclones," and in North and Central America they are called "hurricanes." Depending on where in the world you are exploring, you will need to know the local names. The term "hurricanes" has also become more popularly used in recent times to describe almost all tropical storms.

WHAT IS NEEDED FOR A HURRICANE TO BUILD

Hurricanes can only exist on certain parts of the Earth and at certain times, so most of you are fairly safe. The following things are needed for a hurricane to start to build:

1. Hurricanes form over warm tropical oceans with sea temperatures of at least 78° F/26° C; this temperature must stretch to a depth of around 230 ft./70 m. This is crucial, as warm water is the fuel that feeds a hurricane, so a great depth of water is needed to ensure a sufficient hot water supply.

2. Hurricane season is typically between August and October, when sea temperatures are highest.

3. The area known as the "trade wind belt" allows surface wind to warm as it blows toward the equator. These winds converge or come together in the lower atmosphere, setting up the ideal conditions for hurricane formation.

4. The final key ingredient for hurricane formation is positioning. Hurricanes form between 5 and 20 degrees North and South of the equator. They cannot form any lower than 5 degrees because this is too close to the equator and there simply isn't enough "spin" to get the hurricane turning. After 5 degrees, there is just the right amount of spin (experts call it "Coriolis force").

NATURE'S SPINNING TOPS

Once formed, hurricanes move west and toward the poles. They do this to move extra heat built up at the equator to colder parts of the planet. This is one of the ways in which Earth balances temperatures across the world. Many hurricanes that start out in the warm tropical waters of the Caribbean and Gulf of Mexico end up bringing warming winds and higher temperatures to the United Kingdom and parts of Northern Europe.

The path hurricanes take is very unpredictable. We do know that they generally move to the west and pole-wards but the actual path they take on the way is very shaky. It's a bit like winding up the world's biggest spinning top and letting it go . . . whee!!

HURRICANE STATISTICS

- Hurricanes can grow to a diameter of 400 mi./650 km wide.

- Some experts believe that in one day, a hurricane can release the equivalent amount of energy as half a million atomic bombs.

- Only when a hurricane is fully matured and developed does the famous cloudless, central "eye" form.

- Even though many lives have been lost and many settlements have been destroyed when hurricanes hit land, once a hurricane moves from the ocean onto a land surface it begins to "die." Hurricanes depend on a ready supply of warm water, which is not available on land surfaces. Also, the friction between the hurricanes and land features is much greater than that experienced when a hurricane is over the ocean.

REALLY HORRID HURRICANES

- In November 1998, Hurricane Mitch tore through Central America, causing almost 20,000 deaths; it also caused 20 percent of the Honduran population to lose their homes and destroyed fifty of the main bridges in Nicaragua.

- In November 1970, a tropical cyclone brought winds of more than 125 mi./200 km per hour and hit the crowded Ganges Delta where

300,000 people died, half a million cows drowned and 60 percent of all fishing fleets were lost.

- Hurricane Katrina struck Louisiana on the 29th of August 2005, and made its way into the history books as the most expensive natural disaster in American history with a total estimated property damage of $81 billion.

WHY ARE HURRICANES SUCH DEADLY HAZARDS?

Hurricanes are one of Earth's most deadly hazards because of their size and scale, but it is also because they are more than just hot air. Let's look at the ways in which hurricanes can get you:

High winds—Hurricane-strength winds can often exceed 100 mi./160 km per hour and in extreme cases they can get up to 190 mi./300 km per hour. At that stage, a person would simply be blown away, electricity and communication lines downed, bridges and villages destroyed, and economic disruption would be huge.

Storm surges—The intense wind action whips up the ocean plus the lower surface pressure allows it to rise. This is a major threat to coastal and low-lying areas like deltas. In the Ganges Delta, Bangladesh, the cause of most deaths is a hurricane. The 1970 hurricane mentioned before created a storm surge up to 26 ft./8 m high!

Floods—Whether by storm surges or just the intense rainfall that hurricanes bring, floods brought by hurricanes are another risk factor. In 1974 in Honduras, 800,000 people died as their poorly built houses simply washed away in hurricane floods.

Land and mudslides—These can also result due to heavy rainfall, especially in poorer countries where buildings have been built on steep, unstable slopes and with little or no building codes. Problems are often made worse by deforestation, which exposes the soil, making it easier to slide and slip during intense storms.

SURVIVAL TIPS

1. Luckily, hurricanes are one of the few hazards that can give you some warning. Scientists monitor hurricane-prone areas and can inform radio and television stations when they form. Once you are aware that a hurricane is on its way, you need to prepare.

2. If the area you live is advised to evacuate, it is best to do that. Put away any loose objects around your house. Lock all doors and windows. Turn off the gas, get packed up quickly and hit the road.

3. If you are staying behind, planning is the key to help you defy disaster. Keep a stock of food and household items for emergency purposes and make sure you have a first-aid kit as well as a radio (battery powered is best, in case the power supply goes down).

4. Cover windows and doors with plywood to protect them from winds and flying objects.

5. Fill tanks and containers with water in case supplies are cut off. If you have no containers, fill the bathtub with water so that you have a sufficient supply, but it is more useful to use containers, as the bathtub is a great place to hide during the hurricane. Additional protection can come from covering it with a wooden board once you are inside.

6. During the hurricane, keep away from windows and doors and gather everyone in an interior room of the building. Listen for broadcasts and information on your radio.

7. Do not go outside until you are told that it's safe to leave. Don't be fooled if the hurricane subsides and appears to be over. This is just the perfectly calm "eye" of the storm, which means that it's only halfway finished.

8. After the event, be careful outside as there can still be dangerous hazards such as fires, partially collapsed trees and fallen power cables.

Dreadful Droughts

Drought is a hazardous weather condition that occurs when the climate is drier than it normally would be. Seasonal rains may fail to arrive for months, and sometimes run into years. Rivers and streams begin to dry up and the water held behind dams starts to evaporate. Underground supplies of water can also run out and crops may fail. Ultimately, human, plant and animal existence is seriously threatened by drought. Unlike other hazards, droughts are slow growing and it is difficult to mark off start and finish points.

HOTSPOTS

Drought can strike in most places because the causes of drought vary greatly, but the likelihood is that droughts occur in regions where rainfall is unreliable. Globally, the areas that suffer most from drought include the Great Plains of the United States, the Sahel area of Africa, and Australia.

WHAT CAUSES DROUGHT?

We already know that drought occurs when there is less rainfall than normal. Here are some of the causes behind strange weather events like droughts:

1. El Niño—In the southern hemisphere, every 5–7 years scientists have noticed that the normal pattern of weather reverses over the Pacific Ocean. Warming sea surface temperatures in the Eastern Pacific bring violent storms, rain and mudslides to places that have hardly received any rain for years in parts of South America. Across the Pacific, parts of Australia and Indonesia face deadly droughts when they should be in their rainy season. The crazy meteorological confusion is called the El Niño, meaning the Baby Jesus, because it normally begins around Christmastime.

2. Did you see the ITCZ?—The ITCZ, or Inter-Tropical Convergence Zone, is an area where surface air meets and then rises in the tropics. It is an area that brings major bands of clouds and rain. During the year, the location of the ITCZ varies as it moves north and south of the equator, following the seasonal movement of the overhead sun. If the ITCZ does not move far enough north or south as it normally would, then large areas, especially in Africa, do not receive their normal rainfall. It is also possible that this could happen for several years.

3. Changes in the paths of mid-latitude depressions—The United

Kingdom's total rainfall, for example, is largely brought by bands of clouds and rain called "depressions." If these are displaced by a block of high-pressure air for some time, then a drought can occur even in typically cooler areas. These blocks of "heavier" air mean air cannot rise to form clouds. So, skies are clear, sunny and without rain. The United Kingdom was affected by droughts in the late 1980s and early 1990s due to blocking anticyclones, which divert rain systems away to the north and south.

HISTORIC DROUGHTS

Droughts have been written about and recorded since Biblical times. Some happened so long ago that only estimates to the loss of life can be made. Here are some of the worst famines on record:

DATE	PLACE	NUMBER OF DEATHS
436 BC	Rome, Italy	Estimates in thousands
AD 1586	England	Estimates in thousands
AD 610–1619 * *There were 610 years of drought during this period	Large regions of China	Estimates in millions
AD 1692–94	France	2 million people
AD 1708–1711	East Prussia	250,000 people
1890s 8 drought years in succession	India	Estimates in millions

DATE	PLACE	NUMBER OF DEATHS
AD 1876–79	China	Between 9–13 million people
AD 1983–85	Africa	500,000 people

THE EFFECTS OF DROUGHT

Reduced water supply—The lack of rain combined with lots of evaporation caused by the hot sun means river levels fall and stores of water beneath the ground and in the soil are also reduced.

Crop failure—As water supplies dwindle and moisture in the soil evaporates, then crops have insufficient supplies and could fail, which can have crippling effects on jobs.

Famine—This can then result as crops fail. Food supplies run out and people may die from starvation.

DROUGHT BUSTERS

Nature has created some drought-proof plants and animals that have brilliant design features to defy long periods without rainfall.

Xerophytic (pronounced "zero-fi-tik") plants—A cactus is an excellent example of a xerophytic plant. It has adapted with a waxy coating and small needle-like leaves to reduce the amount of water it loses. The cactus also has long roots to maximize water uptake from deep below the ground.

Pyrophytic (pronounced "pie-row-fi-tik") plants—These are actually fireproof. They can withstand man-made or natural bush fires. The baobab tree of Africa can store large amounts of water in its trunk but has a fireproof bark.

The "ship of the desert"—The camel is perfectly designed for drought conditions. Its thick coat actually reflects sunlight to keep it cool. It has long eyelashes to keep sand and dust out of its eyes. Some myths state that camels carry water in their humps, but it is actually a fatty store that acts as a food supply.

SURVIVAL TIPS

All of us can work together to maximize our water supplies and defeat a drought. There are many simple solutions we can do to help:

1. Ration your water—During a drought, only use water when needed and use it wisely. You could shower rather than take a bath.

2. Collecting water—Collect and reuse fresh rainwater that normally just flows down the drain. Large plastic rain catchers or barrels can be found in most hardware stores.

3. Water-efficient flushes—Many bathrooms are now built with water-efficient flushes that use much less water.

4. Metering and taxing—Many big cities such as New York now meter or tax water to make sure people use less.

5. Hose pipe bans—During a drought, many countries will put a ban on the use of garden sprinklers and hose pipes to save water. People in government are just not fun!

6. Green gardeners—Some clever gardeners are now using drought-resistant grasses and plants. These species actually need a lot less water than other species.

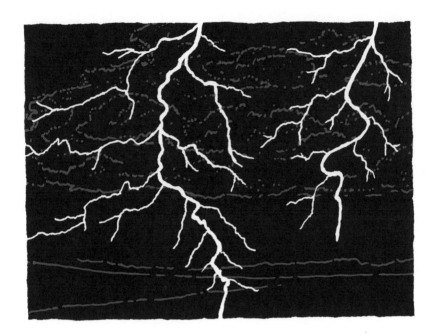

Lightning Storms

Lightning storms can start when warm, moist air meets colder air. The warm air is forced upward, forming giant, towering clouds. Tiny ice crystals inside the clouds crash into each other generating static electricity (you may have done this by rubbing a balloon on your clothes). The top of the cloud becomes positively charged, while the bottom becomes negatively charged. Electricity crackles between the positively charged top and negatively charged bottom of the cloud, shooting to the ground as lightning. The rumble or cracking sound of thunder is caused by the intense heat and expansion of air along the path of the lightning.

WHAT YOU MUST DO

Getting struck by lightning can be a very unpleasant experience, even life-threatening. It is one of the most power-ful forces in nature, and a single strike can zap you with millions of volts of electricity.

Even if the strike does not hit you directly, you may still be in danger from fires and burn-ing that the strikes can ignite. It is unlikely that you will not have any warning of a storm coming. You should see it in the distance and hear the crack of thunder as it approaches.

1. If possible, get indoors as soon as you hear the sound of thunder. Lightning bolts shoot out about 10 mi./16 km from the storm.

2. Once inside, you must avoid electrical equipment. Computers and phones are directly connected to electricity lines and lightning can travel through these and get to you.

3. If you are outdoors, your clothing my save you. Rubber-soled shoes prevent electricity being conducted to you.

4. Stay away from trees and power lines, which can easily conduct the electricity toward them.

5. Take off any metallic items you are wearing, such as belts and keys. These can get very hot and result in serious burns if hit.

6. As the storm passes over you, pull your legs into your chest and make yourself as small as possible. This reduces your size and chances of being hit by lightning.

TRIVIA Lightning bolts are less than 2 in./5 cm wide but burn hotter than the surface of the sun.

YOUNG SCIENTIST ACTIVITY
Make Your Own Static Electricity

EQUIPMENT NEEDED:

Someone's head (with hair)

A wool sock or sweater

Two blown-up balloons

INSTRUCTIONS:

1. Take the two blown-up balloons and rub both against the wool fabric of either a sweater or sock. Now try moving the balloons together. Notice how they force one another apart.

2. Next, rub one of the balloons back and forth on your hair (or someone else's). The best results can be seen with longer hair. Now, slowly pull the balloon away from the hair. The result should be a very bad hair day!

Science Factoid

The balloon experiment works because both the balloons became negatively charged after they were rubbed against the wool material. These negatively charged particles cause the balloons to repel one another and force them apart. Rubbing a balloon against a wool object or someone's hair creates a type of electricity called "static" electricity. This type of electricity causes negatively charged particles (or electrons) to jump to positively charged objects. When you rub the balloons against someone's hair or the wool fabric, they become negatively charged. They have taken some of the electrons from the hair or fabric and left them with a positive charge . . . SHOCKING!!

YOUNG SCIENTIST ACTIVITY
Make a Torch in Your Mouth

You can create your own lightning strikes with your jaws and a packet of candies. This experiment shows you exactly how to create sparks of light just by chewing on good old-fashioned Wint-O-Green Life Savers mints.

EQUIPMENT NEEDED:

One packet of Wint-O-Green Life Savers mints

A very dark place (either indoors or outside)

Your mouth (preferably with real teeth!)

A hand-held mirror

INSTRUCTIONS:

1. Take your packet of Wint-O-Green Life Savers mints into a very dark room or outdoors if it is dark (with no moonlight).

2. Wait a few minutes for your eyes to fully adjust to the darkness.

3. Pop a couple of the candies in your mouth with one hand while positioning the hand-held mirror directly in front of your mouth with the other hand. This will let you see the reaction for yourself.

4. Now, it's crunch time. Begin chewing and notice what happens as you do.

Science Factoid

So, how does this crazy light show work? Well, one of the main ingredients in the Wint-O-Green Life Savers is wintergreen oil. The other is sugar. As you chew, you grind the candies and create an electrical charge. This is what scientists' call tribo-luminescence, a process that makes light when something is torn, ripped, rubbed or crushed.

Flash Floods

In the last 150 years, floods have killed more than 5 million people. Your chance of being flooded depends on where you live. Historically, the most common place on Earth for flood risk is China. In the future, global warming means more people than ever will be vulnerable to the risk of flooding. Humans have covered huge areas of land in concrete and cut down trees. This means that water is washed more quickly into rivers, rather than soaking into the ground. If the climate warms, melting the polar ice caps, higher sea levels and more rain will mean larger areas of land will be affected by flooding.

WHY ARE FLOODS SO DANGEROUS?

You've probably seen images of floods on television. These natural disasters can be very costly, not to mention dangerous. A powerful flood can sweep everything away, from rocks and trees to cars and houses. Foul-smelling water sweeps into buildings and damages property. On a bigger scale, everything from roads to crops and electricity lines may be destroyed. Although there's plenty of water around, you wouldn't want to drink it, as it's often contaminated with sewage and could make you very ill. Accessing food and clean water can be a real problem—that's if you can get somewhere safe and dry. Even when floodwater drains away, it can be months or years before an area recovers.

TRIVIA Flooding is the most common natural hazard on Earth and claims more lives, causes more injuries, and creates more economic and social problems than any other natural event.

RIVER SPELLING CHALLENGE

The Mississippi River can be a pain for two reasons. One, it floods at regular intervals, and two, it is one of the most commonly misspelled rivers in the world.

Most people find it almost impossible to remember and place correctly Mississippi's four Ss, four Is and two Ps. A simple way to navigate this tongue-twister is to imagine a group of ladies sipping tea on its riverbanks. Those present at the tongue-tangled tea party are:

Mrs. M . . . Mrs. I . . . Mrs. SSI . . . Mrs. SSI . . . Mrs. PPI

M. . . I . . . SSI . . . SSI . . . PPI

SURVIVAL TIPS

A flash flood is a large, but temporary, increase in the amount of water passing through a river.

1. Given the rapid onset of flash floods, your warning time will be short and you may have little time to prepare.

2. As with most natural hazards, getting above them is your main aim. Move to high ground quickly.

3. If you are in a vehicle—get out of it! Even small volumes of water are powerful, and staying inside a car will increase your chances of being swept away.

4. Indoors or outdoors, you need to be wary of electrocution from downed power lines or faulty electrics.

5. Fill bathtubs and containers with water as a back-up supply. After a flood, water supplies can become contaminated as sewage systems fail or drowned animals begin to decompose. This water will make you very ill if you drink it (at the very least, you will barf)!

YOUNG SCIENTIST ACTIVITY
Making Bendy Water

This cool little experiment shows the power of static electricity on water. It works on the same principle of the earlier static experiment and you don't need much equipment.

EQUIPMENT NEEDED:

Someone's head (with hair)

A tap with running water

One fully blown-up balloon

INSTRUCTIONS:

1. Find a kitchen or bathroom sink. Turn on the tap so that a stream of water is flowing (the key is to ensure that the stream is more than a few droplets but not a large gush of water). Play around with it until you get a gentle stream.

2. Next, take the blown-up balloon and rub it vigorously through your hair (or someone else's) about 10–12 times.

3. Now bring the balloon across to the water stream. Get very close but be careful not to touch the water. What happens?

Science Factoid

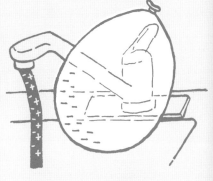

When the balloon is rubbed quickly against the hair, it generates static electricity. This static actually acts on the water molecules and attracts the water toward it. This causes the bending of the water.

Electrons that are negatively charged particles transfer from the hair to the balloon during the rubbing process.

Water has both positive- and negative-charged particles, which are attracted to one another. So, when you bring the balloon close to the water, it draws the water's positively charged particles toward it—you've just made bendy water!

TRIVIA   When the Rio Negro and the Rio Solimoes in Brazil first meet, their waters don't mix with one another for many miles. There is a visible separation of the two rivers, which is easily observed as the Negro's waters are black in color and the Solimoes' are brown in color.

Wildfires

Wildfires are outdoor fires that are, well . . . running wild. They can be very destructive forces of nature and their unpredictability makes them even more deadly for both human and nature populations.

WILDFIRE INGREDIENTS

Wildfires at ground level can travel at great speed, killing plants, wildlife and humans. They will destroy almost everything in their path, burning plant litter, grasses and trees. Some scientists have recorded ground temperatures in wildfires in excess of 1,832° F/1,000° C. That's hotter than the molten rock that erupts from volcanoes!

The perfect equation for a wildfire is: Dry vegetation + Dry air + Wind = Wildfire.

How big or deadly the wildfire becomes will depend on a number of factors, including the climate and type of plants involved, but if dry plants are the fuel for wildfires, then wind is the engine that drives it. The largest wildfires recorded have happened on dry, windy days with low humidity (science-speak for dry air). Wind drives the fires forward, blowing sparks and embers of fire onto new vegetation. The natural whirling and swirling of wind makes tracking and containment of wildfires extremely difficult.

WORLD WILDFIRE FACTS

- Australia experiences more than 15,000 wildfires each year. That's an average of more than 40 fires per day!

- In June and July 1998, wildfires in Florida needed over 5,000 firefighters to put out blazes. Many were flown in from all over the United States.

- Huge fires raged through Indonesia between September 1997 and April 1998, destroying more than 1,160 mi^2/3,004 km^2 of forest (an area larger than the entire landmasses of the Samoan Islands) and over 50,000 people were treated after inhaling smoke-filled air. Pollution reached four times "hazard" level.

- Wildfires are a major concern for farmers in some countries. It is estimated that a whopping $10 million per day is spent in the United States to protect and fight against fires that threaten livestock, crops and timber belts.

- One of Australia's worst fire periods happened on the 16th of February 1983. It claimed the lives of seventy-two students and more than 8,000 people were made homeless.

CAUSES OF WILDFIRES

Most people don't really understand wildfires, and the media often links them with only negative or bad outcomes, but they are actually a natural process in some ecosystems and can be essential and even beneficial at times. Wildfires can be started naturally by lightning strikes. Similarly, man-made wildfires have been fanning around since the earliest farmers first started ploughing, planting and harvesting. In Southern Europe and the Savanna Grasslands of Africa, fire is a key part of both natural ecosystems and man's farming techniques. Here are a few more benefits:

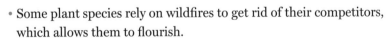

- Some plant species actually need fire to aid in their seed germination. In Australia, the Banksia plant needs fire for its fruit to open and germinate.

- Farmers in Africa's Savanna grasslands deliberately burn fields of vegetation so that the nutrients in the remaining ash are returned to the soil and then help improve the next year's harvest.

- Some plant species rely on wildfires to get rid of their competitors, which allows them to flourish.

- Other species have adapted to defy the threat of fire by developing fire-resistant qualities such as fireproof bark.

EFFECTS

The impact of wildfires can be very wide ranging. If you are near one you will know. The flames can be quite high, the air will make it difficult to breathe, and the sound of tindery, dry wood cracking and flames raging will be almost deafening, not to mention the vast amount of heat that is given off. Some effects include:

Toxic gas pollution—Large amounts of smoke, soot and dust are generated by these reckless blazes. The Indonesian blazes of 1997–98 produced so much smoke that a cloud stretching 1,860 mi./3,000 km from east to west (roughly the size of Western Europe) spread across Southeast Asia and altered weather patterns.

Wildlife losses—Many animals are lost every year due to wildfires. The 2009 fires that struck Victoria, Australia, are believed to have killed millions of animals including kangaroos, koalas, lizards and birds. Kangaroos are especially vulnerable because of their territorial nature. Many suffered badly burned feet after they returned to their habitats shortly after the fires.

Loss of life and property—Fortunately, humans are getting a little better at working with and predicting natural hazards, but some fires move fast and people can get trapped or have their escape routes blocked. Also, some major cities have now expanded into areas that are at risk from fire. Los Angeles and Sydney are key examples where the costs of fighting fires and repairing their damage can run into hundreds of millions of dollars.

Damage to soil—With temperatures ranging anywhere from 1,112° F/ 600° C to more than 1,832° F/1,000° C, these levels of heating can actually change the soil and how it works, which can create major problems for plants, animals and humans.

SURVIVAL TIPS

1. Firefighters talk about creating a "defensible space." If you are at home, a defensible space can reduce the wildfire risk to your home. By removing flammable materials such as branches and leaves in the immediate vicinity of your home, you will reduce the risk of it burning down.

2. Have your radio and television on for the latest news on the situation.

3. Turn off things that will fuel the fire, such as gas and propane.

4. Never drive to an area where a wildfire has already started. They are too unpredictable and deadly to take such a risk.

5. If outside, have protective clothing with you. Long-sleeved tops and long pants are best. To help you breathe, use a handkerchief or scarf to reduce smoke.

6. If your worst fears come true and you are caught outdoors in a wildfire, find a hollow or ditch in the ground. Remove all flammable materials nearby, such as grasses and leaves. This will remove one of the wildfire fuel sources. Get right down into the ditch and cover your face with your hands.

TRIVIA Some countries that are prone to wildfires will go to surprising lengths to protect their trees. The location of Wollemi pine trees in Australia are kept secret. These trees are so rare, that scientists who wish to study them are blindfolded before being taken to see them.

YOUNG SCIENTIST ACTIVITY
The Fireproof Balloon

Balloons are one of the key ingredients for good fun. You can pop them with pins, trod on them or fill them with water. Balloons work so well at bursting because the rubber they are made from is very delicate, but with this experiment you are going to put a balloon in direct contact with fire without bursting it. All you need is a little skill and daring.

EQUIPMENT NEEDED:

One set of matches (adult permission and supervision necessary)

A cup of water • Two equal-sized balloons

INSTRUCTIONS:

1. Blow up the first balloon. Hold the end and tie it.

2. Take the second balloon. Pour half a cup of water inside this balloon. Now blow up the balloon and tie it.

3. Carefully light a match and hold it below the first balloon and let the flame come in contact with the rubber. What happens?

4. Now do the same with the second balloon that contains the water. This time the balloon doesn't burst and you should even find a burn mark on the underside of the balloon to prove that the flame was in contact with it.

Science Factoid

This experiment proves that air and water absorb heat at different rates. The balloon with just air inside heats up very quickly and bursts but the water inside the other balloon absorbs the heat without really raising its temperature at all. This prevents the balloon from being damaged or bursting.

Dreadful
Beasts

Killer Bees

Killer bees, or Africanized honey bees (by their real name), were actually created by accident after a mix-up by a replacement beekeeper in Brazil. The silly snooze released just twenty-six Tanzanian queen bees, which interbred with honeybees from Europe and southern Africa, resulting in the greatly feared killer bee.

Strangely, the killer bee's venom is actually no more potent than that of a normal honey bee, but it is the aggressive "pack" nature of the killer bee that makes it so deadly.

Killer bees have a greater instinct to defend their hive than common honeybees. Scientists call them "hyper-defensive," so they are always on high alert to a potential attack. In reality, they are bees in a really bad mood.

Colonies have a higher proportion of "guard" bees within the hive and they are all too willing to attack. Killer bees swarm more often and in greater numbers than other bee types. The aggressive swarms can and have resulted in human fatalities.

SURVIVAL TIPS

1. If chased by a swarm, the best thing to do is run. Your first 600 ft./200 m are crucial—after that distance, the swarm will start to reduce.

2. While running, try to protect your eyes, nose and mouth. Killer bees believe in getting in headshots! Your hands pressed over your face (with just enough space to see) are a good, makeshift "shield." As long as the bees can be kept from obstructing your vision or breathing, a few dozen stings can easily be managed.

3. Diving into a swimming pool or hiding in a bush will only get you stung to death. Once annoyed, the bees will vigorously patrol their territory for hours stinging anything they encounter. So, unless you've got a suit of armor to spare or an oxygen tank, I wouldn't try either of the above.

4. Strangely, the most likely place to find a swarm of killer bees is not in some remote, wild corner of the countryside, but in cities. The greater availability of flowers and water make our man-made oases much more attractive prospects for these tiny, genetic Frankensteins.

5. Barring an allergic reaction, an able adult should be able to withstand 300–400 stings . . . OUCH!!

Bee and wasp stings are completely different. Wasp stings are alkaline or base. These stings need an acid like vinegar or lemon juice to neutralize the sting, while bee stings are the total opposite. They are acidic and need to be neutralized with something alkaline such as bicarbonate of soda. The next activity lets you test regular household items to see if they are acid or base.

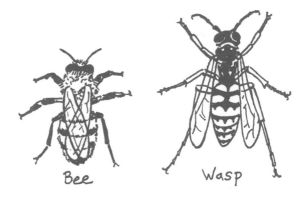

Bee

Wasp

YOUNG SCIENTIST ACTIVITY
Kitchen Color Foamer

Using a range of common kitchen products and an ordinary red cabbage, you can conduct your own test on some of the things you use and eat every day, and make bubbling colored foam as you go.

EQUIPMENT NEEDED:

One glass • One plate

Vinegar • Baking Soda

A jar of pickled red cabbage

INSTRUCTIONS:

1. Open the jar of pickled red cabbage and pour the juice into the glass.

2. Take the plate and pour a small drop of the juice onto it.

3. Sprinkle a tiny amount of the baking soda over the cabbage juice and watch what happens (red juice + white baking soda = green foam).

4. Now add some vinegar to the green foam and see what you get (pink foam).

5. You can experiment with different household products.

Science Factoid

The natural coloring in the red cabbage juice works as an acid-based indicator. It contains a chemical that changes color when it comes in contact with different substances. The vinegar, which is an acid, turns it red. The baking soda, which is a base, turns it green. Adding a little vinegar to the green foam leaves it somewhere in between with a pink color.

Jellyfish Attacks

The box jellyfish—aka the bell jellyfish, the marine stinger or the sea wasp—is one of the deadliest creatures on Earth. Looking at this translucent blob, you would be forgiven for thinking it harmless, but the venom from this little guy can kill you in just over four minutes.

HOW AND WHY

The box jellyfish injects its victim via its numerous tentacles. (Most have more than 50 tentacles, which can be more than 12 ft./3 m long and practically invisible.) They are not aggressive predators, and they certainly don't go on the look out for humans to attack; however, due to their delicate body design (i.e., the fact that they are nothing more than a jellied blob), they can be easily damaged or killed by their prey as they try to fend off an attack. Thanks to evolutionary science, the box jellyfish is now armed with one of the most toxic and deadly chemicals on the planet. This super-strength mix of toxins is designed to kill the box jellyfish's prey instantaneously and thereby nullify any possible fight. Each tentacle has thousands of tiny stinging darts along its entire length that are automatically triggered by chemical reactions caused when the tentacle comes in contact with a fish or, worse, a human.

TRIVIA

- The "box" or "bell" jellyfish gets its name from its body shape, which resembles those items.

- Scientists estimate that one jellyfish packs enough venom to kill up to sixty grown adult humans.

- Historical records attribute more than one hundred deaths to the box jellyfish.

- The toxins released by a box jellyfish also attack the skin and can leave victims with blackened skin and permanent scarring.

- People stung in open water often die from a heart attack or go into shock before they even reach dry land.

SURVIVAL TIPS

Believe it or not, there is quite a bit you can do to keep yourself harm-free, but you may have to compromise both your wardrobe and your manliness (if you are a male). If you are a female, you might not mind at all! Look at these tips:

1. Find their stomping ground—Most box jellyfish are concentrated in the waters around Australia, the southern Pacific and Indonesia.

2. Anti-venom—Scientists have discovered an anti-venom and it is widely available. Pack a dose of it with you to counteract the sting. Alternatively, you can use an acetic acid-like vinegar to help, but you will need to be quick since shock, nausea, vomiting, breathing problems or worse can quickly set in. The vinegar quickly sets about neutralizing the toxin, therefore reducing its ferocity and the danger.

3. Pack a pair of pantyhose—Yes, I said pantyhose. You may feel ridiculous and even a little weird, but Australian lifeguards have been using this little scientific trick for years. They realized the nylon in the pantyhose prevented the jellyfish from detecting the chemicals in their skin and therefore the jellyfish didn't sting them. Pantyhose or death? I don't think there is much debate, mister!

YOUNG SCIENTIST ACTIVITY
How to Make Fake Boogers

Although potentially deadly, in reality, jellyfish are no more than gooey blobs of protein similar to your boogers. Boogers are one of the body's natural proteins, and, using this experiment, you can re-create them to use in any situation you see fit, and with the right amount of food coloring, you can make your boogers a perfectly disgusting shade of green.

EQUIPMENT NEEDED:

A jug of warm water • Some Borax laundry soap

Green food coloring • Some Elmer's glue

Two large bowls • One cup and some tablespoons

INSTRUCTIONS:

1. Pour 2 cups/0.5 L of warm water into one of the bowls.

2. Mix in ⅛ cup of Borax laundry soap and leave the mixture time to cool a little.

3. Take the other bowl and mix in three spoonfuls of water and two spoonfuls of glue. Now add a few drops of food coloring and mix until you are happy with the color.

4. Take a spoonful of the Borax mixture and add it to the glue and food coloring. You've just made fake boogers ... enjoy!

Science Factoid

Although the proteins and sugars in your fake boogers are different from those made by your body, they work in the same way and have similar characteristics. Typically, they are sticky substances that gather along stretchable strands. If you've got your mixtures right, you should have green, stringy-stretchy boogers that look and act like the real thing so no one "nose" the difference!

Alligators

WRESTLING AN ALLIGATOR

Today, there are only a small number of professional alligator wrestlers left, but the art form itself dates back to a time when Native Americans would capture alligators with their bare hands as a means of food supply. But be warned—this is a very risky exercise that requires skill, speed and quick thinking. Having said that, once trained, this skill could be a lifesaver.

SURVIVAL TIPS

If you have never wrestled an alligator before, there are a number of precautions you need to take to ensure you don't end up minus a body part.

1. Find a professional alligator wrestler—This is the safest and best place to start. Alligator wrestlers know all the pros and cons of tackling an alligator, and they will give you the top tips you need to succeed.

2. Start small—It is best to hone your skills on a small alligator first. These are easier to handle and are less powerful, which puts you in a much stronger position!

ADVANCED WRESTLING

Once you feel confident enough to take on a full-grown alligator in the wild, there are a few simple but important steps to follow:

1. Always approach from behind—Never approach from the front or side. You will most likely get bitten. Coming from behind makes it difficult for the alligator to see you.

2. Put your shirt on it—Remove your shirt or t-shirt and throw it over the alligator's head, ensuring that its eyes are covered. Without vision, the alligator's reactions will be slower.

3. From directly behind the alligator, get a running start and leap onto the animal with hands extended forward. Make sure your hands land on the alligator's neck, between the back of its jaws and the front legs. Draw in your legs and body weight to straddle the main body of the animal to pin it in place.

4. Control the mouth—Once on the gator, maintain pressure on the head and force it toward the ground to prevent its jaws from opening. Now slide your hands forward, down to the bottom jaw line. Clasp your fingers and thumbs under the jaw and grip firmly. You should now be using both hands to hold the jaw shut.

5. Your final move—With all your strength, lift the alligator's head off the ground and raise it to roughly a ninety-degree angle. Once you have gotten to this point, the gator is beaten . . . well done,

you've now wrestled your first alligator . . . there's just one small catch . . . getting off!

6. The dismount—This is difficult because you have to get to your feet, maintain pressure on the alligator's body and keep your balance. The simplest technique is to work back through your approach steps. Keep pressure on the head and body. Apply pressure to the head and neck while drawing your feet up to dismount. Your aim is to throw the alligator forward while you jump back. This will put maximum distance between you. Even after this, the gator may turn on you. Move away quickly in a straight line and be prepared to run. The gator will quickly tire and drop away.

Whales

HOW TO ESCAPE FROM A WHALE'S BELLY

To be honest with you, being swallowed whole by a whale is most unlikely. Yes, there are some accounts by sailors that they were swallowed by whales and then promptly spat back out into the ocean again, but whether such stories are true or not have yet to be proved. Instead, it is the massive size of these peaceful creatures that could really put you in trouble.

Whale watchers, sailors and scientists have always been eager to witness the curious behaviors of these giant marine animals, but would you know what to do if you encountered one of Earth's biggest

creatures? Would you know what to do if you witnessed the spectacular sight of a whale "breaching"? Could you tell the difference between
a "spy hop" and "lobtailing"? Would you understand the meaning of
a "bubble trail"? If the answer to any of these questions is no, then
you can pat yourself on the back for being smart enough to have this
book in your possession. You're about to discover some of nature's
best-kept secrets.

WHALE TOP TIPS

Spy Hopping

Spy hopping is a very clever and controlled behavior carried out by
whales. It involves the whale raising its head vertically out of the water
and holding itself there, sometimes for several minutes. Some experts
describe it as the whale equivalent of humans treading water and just
as the name implies, "spy hopping" gives the whale time to take a good
look around.

Lobtailing

Lobtailing involves a whale lifting its tail (or flukes) out of the water
before bringing it down onto the surface of the water very quickly and
with great force to produce a loud
"slap." Most species do this many
times in a row, and experts believe
the sounds and the visual impact of
this practice are a smart means of communication used by whales to speak to one
another. Be careful though, if you are in a
boat nearby when this happens, it could generate waves large enough to knock you
overboard.

Beware of Breaching!

Breaching is a truly spectacular sight and involves these enormous creatures launching themselves out of the ocean, spinning in the air and returning back under the surface. Breaching can be carried out by a single whale or in a group, and it often involves a large number of repeated jumps. Although it is an amazing sight to behold, it can be very dangerous. Some explorers have even ended up being struck by a breaching whale!

Brilliant Bubble Trails

Whale experts describe bubble trailing as a very cute trick whales use to hide themselves from competitors. It involves a whale releasing a long, controlled stream or trail of bubbles from its blowhole to leave a long path of beautiful bubbles behind. This dazzling display often occurs in competitive groups, and it is believed that this bubbling behavior acts as a visual screen, making it difficult for other whales to see an opponent underwater.

BIZARRE BREACHES

In 2010, a couple on a whale-watching trip off Cape Town, South Africa, had a lucky escape when a 33 ft./10 m southern right whale weighing forty tons leapt onto their yacht. Luckily, neither the passengers nor the whale were really injured.

In 2009, a fishing boat almost sank off the coast of Cabo San Lucas, Baja California, after it collided into a breaching whale. The shocked captain managed to get his vessel back to shore, but could not believe that his boat had withstood the collision with the forty-ton giant, which lifted the crew approximately 4 ft./1 m in the air!

Whale who stopped a race—In 2011, 3 mi./4 km off Cape Disappointment, Oregon, the crew of the sailboat *L'Orca* was competing in the Oregon International Offshore Race when a whale with a little bad timing ended their participation in the competition. The whale, believed to be a humpback, slammed down the boat, destroying the mast and the rigging of the vessel. The crew had to be towed back to safety by the U.S. Coast Guard. Miraculously, no crew members were hurt, but the whale was left with a few small scratches as it left behind some small pieces of blubber and a barnacle.

Poison Dart Frogs

Poison dart frogs may look small, cute and colorful but they can sure unleash a whole world of pain. Found in the tropical forests of South America, these guys are very bright and come in an array of tones, including red, blue, gold and green.

The most deadly frog of them all is the tiny, 2-in./5-cm-long golden poison dart frog. Scientists believe that one adult carries enough poison to kill as many as 20,000 mice and 10 adult humans.

GOLDEN POISON DART FROGS

Scientists believe poison dart frogs get their toxins from their diet. They live on insects, which, in turn, feed on local toxic plants found in the rainforest. This is proved by the fact that dart frogs bred in captivity don't have any poison. South American Indian tribes used the dart frog poison on their arrowheads and blow darts to kill the animals they were hunting. How deadly is the poison? The poison is strong enough to kill a monkey instantaneously. Laboratory research shows that the lethal dose for an adult human weighing 150 lbs./68 kg would be the equivalent of two fine grains of salt.

The deadly toxin is released from glands behind the frog's ears when they are frightened, stressed or in pain. It appears as a colorless or milky substance. This toxin is a neurotoxin, which means it can mess with brain and nerve signals, causing convulsions, foaming at the mouth, heart failure and ultimately death.

The bright colors the frogs display are for a good reason. This is nature's way of saying "Back off! Don't mess with me." It is a warning to any predator that might be looking for a snack. In the wild, poison dart frogs have one natural predator. The Amazon ground snake has the natural ability to withstand the toxins released by the frogs.

SURVIVAL TIPS

1. In truth, you don't really have many options other than being smart and organized. There is currently no antidote for this type of poisoning, so extra care is paramount.

2. It is said that the poison dart frog has enough toxins to kill 10 men. Some explorers joke that in a large expedition group in the rainforests of South America, the smartest explorer is number 11!

3. In reality, there's a fairly straightforward rule of survival to follow: "Look but don't touch!"

YOUNG SCIENTIST ACTIVITY
The Potato Dart Gun

With the right kit, an explorer will go far. If this kit doubles as a fun game, then even the better. This activity will show you how to make a potato dart gun, which can be used for target practice and lots of other fun games.

EQUIPMENT NEEDED:

One piece of copper pipe

Several large potatoes

A metal nail file

A piece of wooden dowel or a bamboo garden cane

INSTRUCTIONS:

1. Use your file to make sure both ends of the pipe are really smooth.

2. Take one of the large potatoes and place it on the ground.

3. Push the copper pipe into the potato until it goes all the way through. Now do it with the other end of the pipe. You should now have potato at both ends.

4. Take the dowel rod or bamboo cane. Use all your strength to push it inside the copper piping. Your potato dart gun is now "loaded." All you need to do now is find a target, take aim and slam your hand hard on the end of the rod or cane . . . Pop! . . . you've fired your first potato dart!

Science Factoid

With the potato jammed into both ends of the copper pipe, an airtight seal is created. This traps air inside the pipe. As you push one piece of potato along the tube, the space between the two bits of potato gets smaller. This compresses the air inside the pipe and increases pressure. This pressure builds and builds as the air in the tube is compressed until the force exerted onto the potato at the front of the pipe is so great that it overcomes the friction that holds it in place. The potato is then fired out at great speed, just like those shot from poison dart guns!

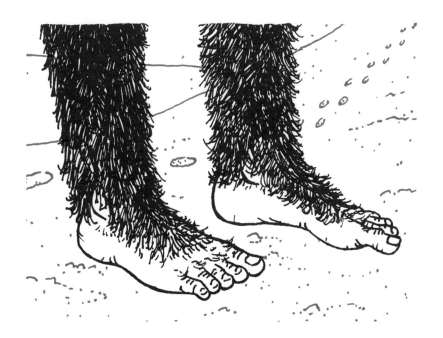

The Abominable Snowman

The Abominable Snowman has a number of aliases that you are best to be familiar with in case you encounter one on your adventures across the globe. Also known as the Yeti, this mysterious creature is thought to be native to the Himalayan mountain range, which crosses the India, Nepal and Tibet regions. However, many experts also believe this mythical creature is linked to the legendary "Sasquatch," aka "Bigfoot," which is said to be native to North America.

BACKGROUND FACTS

Although reports and sightings vary, it is fair to describe the Abominable Snowman and its North American cousin as a large, hairy, ape-like creature that can stand on two legs. Standing at its full height, eyewitness reports describe the Abominable Snowman as ranging in height between 6 and 10 ft./2 and 3 m. A full-grown adult can weigh in excess of 500 lbs./230 kg, and is typically covered in dark brown or dark reddish hair. Described by many as half-man, half-ape, the elusive creature is said to roam only the most remote peaks where humans rarely venture.

TRIVIA As word spread throughout the world about the Abominable Snowman or Himalayan Yeti, the Nepali government cashed in on the increasingly popular story by issuing Yeti-hunting licenses in the 1950s, priced at $600/£400 per Yeti. To date, no one has succeeded in capturing a proven specimen dead or alive.

SURVIVAL TIPS

If you are still adamant that you want to venture to one of the world's coldest, most remote and isolated regions, then you are going to have to be on top of your game. Here are some top survival tips:

1. Have a Sherpa team ready—Sherpa are expert guides with a tradition of escorting explorers through the dangers of the Himalayas. They will help you acclimatize to the mountains, understand the changeable weather and know the best routes. Beware, though, Sherpa fear the Yeti greatly and they will only take you so far if they fear they may anger or simply encounter a Yeti.

2. Bring night-vision goggles—The Yeti is described as a nocturnal creature and so your best chance of a clear sighting will be with a good pair of night-vision goggles.

3. Listen up!—Eyewitnesses claim that the Yeti will whistle, growl and toss rocks aside while foraging for food—so listen carefully.

4. One deadly blow—Legend states that the Yeti will stand up to attack and can kill with a single punch. There are numerous stories of yaks (animals about the size of a bison) being killed by a single blow from a Yeti.

5. Move quickly and beware—Ancient records mention the Yeti's ability to "move swiftly" on "two or four feet," and, more chillingly, they state that they "can only be caught when they are ill or dead."